600

D0627308

DARE TO DREAM

TIM DAGGETT

WITH JEAN STONE

WYNWOOD® Press

A DIVISION OF

Baker Book House

Grand Rapids, Michigan

Copyright ©1992 by Tim Dagget and Jean Stone
Published by Wynwood® Press
a division of
Baker Book House Company
P.O. Box 6287
Grand Rapids, Michigan 49516-6287

ISBN: 0-922066-77-9

Second printing, July 1992

Printed in the United States of America

Library of Congress Cataloging-in-Publication Data

Daggett, Tim.
    Dare to dream : tragedy and triumph : the heroic struggle of an
Olympic champion / Tim Daggett with Jean Stone.
        p.   cm.
    ISBN 0-922066-77-9
    1. Daggett, Tim.   2. Gymnasts—United States—Biography.
I. Stone, Jean.   II. Title.
GV460.2.D34D34   1992
796.44'092—dc20
    [B]   91-28679
                                                          CIP

There are so many special people who have been there for me throughout my life and career, and without them, none of the successes that I had, the obstacles that I overcame, or the inner growth that I experienced would have been possible.

The list is long—you know who you are—please understand that I know I couldn't have done it without you. I also know you know me well enough to understand why I have chosen to dedicate this book

to
Coach Bill Jones
Makoto Sakamoto
Art Shurlock
Yefim Furman
John, Doris, and Peter Vidmar
the guys from the '84 Team . . .

and especially . . .
to my family.

Tim Daggett

To the memory of my parents
Stewart and Miriam Bozenhard,
who encouraged the hope—

And to Tim,
who gave me back the dream.

Jean Stone

CONTENTS

PROLOGUE
The Dream Comes True

"And now . . .
  Tim
  Daggett
  gets
  a
  10!"

ABC commentator Jack Whitaker screamed. The crowd at Pauley Pavilion leaped to their feet, their thundering cheers deafening the broadcast microphones. The arena of over ten thousand erupted into a surging sea of red, white and blue. And families in living rooms all across America jumped from their sofas, hugging one another, squealing with joy.

"They've got it now, guys!" co-commentator Kurt Thomas shouted above the roar, as the kid from West Springfield, Massachusetts, clinched the gold medal for the United States Men's Gymnastics Team.

*   *   *

It was July 31, 1984. More than seven thousand athletes from 140 countries had gathered in Los Angeles for the XXIII Olympic Games. And that night, with the perfect score for my performance on the high bar, the U.S. Men's Gymnastics Team came out on top for the first time since the turn of the century.

For the past year I had practiced that routine with every skill and every move I used that night: the flyaway half, the Stalder positions, the two releases and the full twisting double layout—skills that would mean extra points because of their difficulty—dangerous skills which could mean the difference between the gold, silver, bronze, or no medal at all. In drill after drill, I practiced those skills, practiced "sticking" my dismount over and over and over again.

The high bar was the last event of the team competition. We had been through the floor exercise, the pommel horse, the rings, the vault and the parallel bars. Our team had done exceptionally well, and our scores had us running neck and neck with the Chinese. But we were tired. And the pressure was intense.

I was fifth in the lineup. My closest friend, Peter Vidmar, was last. As we watched our teammates perform, I turned to Peter.

"It's just like we practiced," I said. "We're back in the gym. Pretend we're only there. Just like when we pretended we were here."

I was referring to those late-night hours at the UCLA gym when Peter and I trained with our coach, Makoto "Mako" Sakamoto. Night after night, when the regular workouts were over, we prepared for this moment. Our teammates had gone home, exhausted from the day's training. Peter, Mako and I were alone in the gym, alone with the stillness of the waiting apparatus. We turned off the radio and listened to the quiet. Though we, too, were tired, this was our time. It was the time that would make us better, stronger. It was the time that would turn us into champions. For it was during those after-hours workouts while we disciplined our bodies that we also conditioned our minds, employing visualization techniques which put us, ironically, in the identical position we were in that night. We took turns acting as the commentator.

"It's the last event of the team competition," Peter announced. "Tim Daggett is up next. And he needs a perfect 10 for the team to beat the Chinese."

I imagined Mako as a stern-faced, Eastern bloc judge, and saluted him in pure gymnastics form before mounting the bar. I saw the arena throbbing with anticipation. I heard the excitement of the imaginary crowd. I felt the tension of the illusory competition. I mounted the bar and gave the best performance possible.

Then it was Peter's turn.

"It's the last event of the team competition," I announced. "Peter Vidmar is up next. . . ."

We repeated those routines night after night, workout after workout, bringing the sense of the Olympic arena into the hollow gym. Now that imagery had come to life. We simply had to reenact those routines. But this time, it was for real.

My chance finally came, and I was scared. I saluted the judge, then looked up at the bar. I felt the adrenaline rush through me. I knew that if I got up there and did my very best we could achieve something as a team that had never been done before. I took a deep breath.

"This is it," I thought. "The moment is now." Abie Grossfeld, the head U.S. Olympic Coach for Men's Gymnastics, lifted me up to the bar. I grasped the cold, grainy steel in my palms and—*wham!*—I felt the connection. Nothing was going to tear my grip away. I exploded into my routine, cutting through the air with newfound power, knowing even when I did my release skills that I was still part of the bar, still connected to its strength. Backward. Forward. Bail through the bottom. Swing from the top. I let go of the bar for my dismount. I heard the bar vibrate with success.

"Stick it! Stick it!" I commanded my legs. Then I stuck that dismount cold.

Abie grabbed me around the waist and gave me a huge bear hug.

That was one of the most memorable things anyone ever did. Abie is such a great guy, such an incredible gymnast himself. But it's really out of character for him to show his enthusiasm so publicly. That hug was one of the greatest compliments I could have received.

The 10 was posted. Emotion flooded the arena. And suddenly six hardworking, little-known gymnasts became America's headlines and America's heroes.

"U-S-A! U-S-A!" The chants began with a fury.

I looked up into the stands for my mom. Everything was happening so fast, and it was so loud in there! But strangely, even through all those people, I saw her right away. I don't even think I waved. I just stood there grinning from ear to ear.

The really odd thing is that consciously I had no idea where she was sitting. Even at all the meets and competitions I've been in, I've never tried to find my family in the audience. I was afraid it would distract me to know where they were. Just knowing they *were* there was enough. My family was always so supportive that they accepted that little fear of mine, and always gave me that space. But when I looked up and saw my mom right away, I knew that somewhere deep inside me I had known all along where she was.

There, high in the stands, with five of my brothers and sisters, she was on her feet with the rest of the crowd, waving her flags frantically, tears of joy streaming down her face.

My mother later told a reporter that she doesn't remember what she was thinking. "Excitement, certainly. Pride. And relief. It was such a thrill, so unexpected and so overwhelming. We knew Timmy was doing wonderfully, but we never dreamed he would be the one to clinch the gold.

"Before we knew it, the cameras were on us, and the media crowded around. The media and all kinds of people! They wanted to shake our hands, to congratulate us, to say 'thank you' to the family of the boy who had just made the United States go down in the history books."

I rushed off the platform and gave a high-five to Mitch Gaylord, who was not only a fellow Olympian, but also a UCLA teammate.

I wanted to share the moment with Peter, too, but Peter still had his routine to do, and I didn't want to take away from that. So I just gave him a slap on the back and he knew. He knew.

Later I discovered Peter didn't know.

In team competition, only five of the six scores are used. As the fifth score for the U.S. Men, my 10 had secured the gold. In reality, Peter didn't have to finish his routine, but he was concentrating so intently on being the last one up that he was unaware where the scoring stood. He had shut out the crowd and was focused solely on the performance he had to give. He thought it was all up to him.

When Peter tells people about this today, he laughs as he says, "I wish someone had told me we'd already won!"

I disagree. It wouldn't have been fair to break his concentration. He needed that energy to give the performance of his life. And that's really what gymnastics—and life—is all about: giving it your all.

Peter mounted the high bar and performed a spectacular routine, landing his dismount and scoring a 9.95.

The competition was over. The U.S. Men were officially declared the gold medal winners.

The Chinese came over and congratulated us. That was a really emotional moment, but it was even more meaningful when Li Ning, China's legendary gymnast, shook my hand.

"*Hun hao* (good job)." Li bowed his head slightly.

I looked into his black eyes and saw his sincerity. My god, I thought, this is one of my idols, and we have just beaten him. Then I remembered another time when Li shook my hand with such sincerity.

It was Moscow, 1981, at the World Championships. Recovering from surgery, I was wearing a brace on each ankle.

I heard that Li had sprained his ankle a couple of days before the meet, and that he was wearing some kind of makeshift taping around it. I thought about Li's disappointment if he couldn't compete—he is such a dedicated, extraordinary gymnast. Suspecting that many of the sports medicine techniques in China weren't as advanced as ours, and sensing that my left ankle was pretty well healed, I wanted to give Li one of my braces.

With my pal Peter Vidmar in tow, I explored the vast Soviet sports complex in search of Li Ning.

The complex had been built for the 1980 Olympics, and it was really huge. First we had to find out where the Chinese delegation was housed. We finally found the right elevator and luckily were directed to Li's room right away.

Li's roommate was another great Chinese competitor, Tong Fei. Tong greeted us at the door and welcomed us into the room.

Their room was just like ours: concrete walls, little furniture, with no pictures or other adornments. The carpeting was thin and dark, and we could feel a chill coming from the window. (In fact, in our own room, the air blew so cold that we used athletic tape to seal around the window.)

Tong called out to Li, who woke quickly from a nap. Though neither of them knew English, and neither Peter nor I knew Chinese, we "spoke" with gestures and amateurish sign language—a sort of primitive communications "art form" you learn to adapt after years of being around others who, it seems, always speak a language other than ours!

I pointed to Li's taped foot.

"Your ankle. Just like mine," I said, pointing to my own ankles, where I wore the braces. I bent down and took off the brace from my right ankle. I pointed to Li's ankle again.

"For you. For your ankle."

Li understood. He took the brace and examined it. Then he sat on the edge of the bed and tried to figure out how to put it on. I stooped to help him, showing him the adjustments and how to make sure the fit was secure.

Li smiled and shook my hand vigorously.

"*Shay, shay* (thank you)," he said. "*Hun hao. Hun hao.*"

We started to leave and Tong Fei held up his hand for us to wait. Li Ning, now walking more securely with the brace in place, said something to Tong, and they rifled through their bags. They took out an unopened package of a Chinese delicacy and a box of rice crackers. They handed the gifts to us.

"*Shay, shay*, United States," they said with a smile. And again, they shook our hands.

Li was able to compete after all, even winning a well-deserved medal during the meet. And Peter and I have a wonderful memory of what we feel international relations should be all about.

It was that cold day in Moscow, three years earlier, that I thought of now as Li shook my hand.

I knew that, though disappointed for his team, Li knew how hard we had worked. His words said "good job." And his eyes said, "I'm happy for you, Tim Daggett."

An Olympic volunteer lined up the team to escort us out of the main arena to await the medals ceremony.

When I look back on the videotapes of the seven of us—Peter, Jim Hartung, Bart Conner, myself, Mitch, Scott Johnson and our team alternate, Jim Mikus—parading past the stands, I can still feel the enthusiasm that was inside me. We were laughing, crying, smiling and shouting—none of us could find the right words to say, we just kept uttering unbelievably loud sounds of joy. The volunteer led us into a huge corridor behind the stands, and we did what none of us are able to do very well—we waited.

But we didn't wait quietly. Inside the corridor we could still feel the arena pulsating with the cheering crowd, we could still hear the muffled cheers and screams.

"*U-S-A! U-S-A!*"

We danced around hugging each other and slapping each other on the back. We were totally out of control. We had dreamed of this moment, yet I don't think any one of us could have actually imagined the elation we were feeling.

Then another volunteer came in and took the edge off our excitement.

"Okay, the six team members line up in pairs," he said.

"That's not right!" one of us said. "It's seven, not six." The volunteer had forgotten to include Jim Mikus.

He rechecked the clipboard.

"No. Only the six team members who competed."

This was the first we had heard of the Olympic rule whereby, unlike any other international competition, the team alternate, because he doesn't actually compete in the games, is not a medal recipient.

The alternate is an important facet of the team. Jim, in addition to being a good friend of mine with whom I had competed for many years, was a great gymnast, and had worked very hard to get to the Olympics. His contribution to the team was valuable. Now he was not going to be able to receive a medal. It didn't seem fair. We tried to protest, but the volunteer was adamant. Only the six team members who competed would be on the winners stand.

"Don't worry about me," Jim said. "Just get out there and get your medals."

With spirits a little dampened, our team of six lined up.

That incident really hurt, but we also knew Jim wouldn't want us to make a big deal out of it. I fell into line beside Scott Johnson, took a deep breath, and prepared for our ultimate reward.

This time when we marched into the arena I knew where to look for my mom. I saw her and all the kids waving, and I got an awful lump in my throat. I knew if it hadn't been for my family, I wouldn't be here now. I straightened my back, held back the tears, and kept walking on toward the winners stand.

Ever since I was a little boy I had dreamed of this moment. I had dreamed of the excitement, the thrill of winning the gold. But as I stood on the stand, I was not thinking of the glamour, the glory or our newfound fame. Instead, I was remembering one seemingly inconsequential week of my life—a week of training.

Mako was more than a successful coach, he was a master motivator. One way Mako motivated his athletes was to encourage them to push themselves beyond what they thought possible.

Just before a qualifying meet, Mako and I met at a small coffee shop on the UCLA campus to go over my training schedule. He had singled out one week—a week that would be a most intense, a most difficult, and an almost nearly impossible to accomplish session of rigorous training. When Mako planned these weeks of training, nothing changed the schedule. Not final exams. Not if you got the flu. What you planned, you did. It was that simple.

Though in the years to come I realized the importance of such rigid training, at the time I didn't always think Mako's method was sensible. It seemed a little unrealistic; it seemed somehow wrong. In a competition the greatest number of routines that a gymnast performs is six in one day. During this week we scheduled thirty-six routines a day. And that didn't count warm-ups. It was dangerous, too. Trying to do a triple back somersault off the rings when you're completely exhausted can lead to injury.

"There is a fine line between being a good gymnast and being a champion," Mako said. "You must decide how badly you want to cross that line."

I trusted him, and he was right. In fact, after that week was finally over, I realized I had never felt such satisfaction. Not because I won anything, because I hadn't; but because I had done it. I had done what I set out to do, and because of that, I felt like a champion.

Now, here it was, the Olympics. We had achieved the impossible. We had won the gold. Some people may think it ludicrous that in the heat of the excitement and the thrill of that moment, I was thinking only of such a seemingly insignificant time as that one week of training. But it was because of that week that my commitment had been solidified, and I had proved to myself I could do it. As I stood on the winners stand, the real meaning behind that week became clear—it was not the repetition of the routines that had been important, but the strengthening of my mind, the reinforcement that I could reach my dream. What I didn't realize was the even greater significance that lesson would have later in my career.

"Timothy Daggett," the announcer said clearly.

I bent down to receive the flowers, and the gold was placed around my neck. The crowd exploded again.

"U-S-A! U-S-A!" As each of our names was called, the chants grew louder.

Peter, Bart and Jim were crying—the emotion for them perhaps ran even deeper, as they had been members of the 1980 Olympic team, and had seen their dreams dissolve in President Carter's boycott. Mitch, Scott and I stood with aching, rigid muscles, with smiles of innocence, and maybe even of disbelief. We were a team, but more than that, we had become friends. And during those Olympic Games, we had seen our individual dreams become one.

The flowers and silver medals were presented to the team from the People's Republic of China, the bronze to the Japanese.

Then I stood like a statue, for I knew what was coming next: the raising of the flags and the playing of "The Star-Spangled Banner."

I put my hand over my heart and started to sing. And I knew at that moment I would never again hear our national anthem without being back there, receiving my gold medal and feeling so proud to represent our country. Because I felt then that nowhere but in America could a kid from a small town and a big family, whose father was a school teacher, have the opportunity to try, and be given the chance to have his dream come true.

PART I

THE
DreaM

1

He didn't look like the other Daggett babies. They were blond and fair with light eyes and rosy pink cheeks, indicative of the Irish heritage of both parents. But Timothy had an enormous amount of black, black hair, and, even at birth, his eyes were dark.

"This can't be my baby," I said with certainty as I looked into the hospital nursery. "There must be some mistake."

Lying in the bassinet next to Timothy's was a blond, fair-skinned baby with rosy cheeks. His tag identified him as "Baby Gonzalez."

"That must be Timothy," I said to the doctor who stood by my side.

The doctor smiled. "No, Connie, this little brunette is indeed your baby. I put the ID tags on him myself in the delivery room."

I thought for a moment as I studied the two babies through the glass. I was unconvinced.

Later, when a nurse brought the dark-haired baby to me, a friend was visiting. I confided my doubts.

"How can I ever love this baby when I'm not sure he is mine?" I asked.

My friend leaned over to take a closer look at the tiny bundle.

"Look, Connie, he has John's nose. That perfect little 'A' shape nose. Just like John's. In fact, look at his whole face. He looks exactly like John."

I once again studied the tiny face. My friend was right, he did look like John, my husband. Apparently he was mine, after all.

"Well, little Timothy," I whispered to the sleeping infant. "You certainly aren't starting off like the other children. Which can only mean one thing: because you're so different, you must be someone very special."

—Connie Daggett
Tim's Mother

As time passed my mother was reminded of this many times. The third of what would be seven Daggett children of Connie and John (the later babies were all blond and fair), I apparently began showing just how different I really was at an early age . . . and not always in a positive way! More than once I overheard Mom say to my father, "This kid is going to be the death of me." There was never any doubt *which* kid she was talking about.

When I was still in a crib, I began displaying an unusual quality: I was fearless.

No sooner would my mother tuck me in, and turn around to shut off the light and close the door, than I would be at her feet, sneaking out of the door. I loved climbing up over the rails of my crib and leaping onto the floor. She says she worried about me constantly. She was convinced I was going to hurt myself.

By the time I was five years old, my parents knew I needed something the other kids never did: I needed to be disciplined with a firm hand.

One day she found me crawling to the top of the refrigerator, trying to get at the cereal boxes in the cabinet above. (Why do moms always put the good stuff out of reach?) She whisked me down and screamed at me.

"Oh, oh," I thought.

"I think it's time for an old-fashioned spanking," she said firmly.

She sat at the table, turned me over her knee, and gave my bottom a few good slaps. What I couldn't figure out was why *she* was crying. After all, I was the one getting spanked. Besides, it didn't even hurt!

Anyway, after a few spanks I thought she'd had enough, so I turned and looked up at her. I guess I knew that one look into my big brown eyes would win her over.

"Are you done yet?" I asked quietly, trying to sound as though my feelings had really been hurt.

She looked at me, sighed, then wiped her eyes. I scampered off her lap and went skipping outside.

That night my parents tried to think of some other form of discipline. Conventional methods simply weren't going to work on this kid! They decided to take the approach my mom had seen her mother use on one of her brothers. The next time I did something wrong, she stood me in the corner.

"Stay there and think about what you've done!" she said, convinced this would work. She left the room and returned a few minutes later to find me slumped in the corner.

She rushed over to me.

"Oh, no! What have I done! What's happened to Timmy?" she cried. She quickly bent down and discovered that I had fallen sound asleep. When she talks about my childhood, Mom uses the word "exasperating" a lot.

But I never got into any *real* trouble. I guess I was just always "into things."

Today I would probably have been diagnosed as hyperactive, and I suppose I was. But my parents thought I was just energetic. Wow, was I energetic!

Some days Mom found me on top of the garage roof, ready to jump into a pile of leaves on the ground. Other times I was up a tree somewhere, climbing so high no one could see me.

I loved to hide, and I guess I gave my folks many a scare.

The scariest of which, perhaps, was one Memorial Day when I was seven years old.

We lived in West Springfield, Massachusetts, a small town rich in

the traditions of Old New England. Among these is the annual celebration of Memorial Day—complete with a parade of the local school
bands, the Boy Scouts, the Girl Scouts and the American Legion.
Each year my parents packed the seven of us kids into the station
wagon and drove to the center of town to watch the parade. We went
to my mom's parents' home off Elm Street for the best view.

That year when the kids piled out at Grandma and Grandpa's, Mom
took a head count for balloon-buying, and to make sure we were all out
of the car.

"One, two, three, four, five, six . . ."

She counted again, then frantically began scanning faces.

"My god, where's Timothy?" she shrieked.

They rechecked the car. I was nowhere to be seen.

My father jumped back into the station wagon and drove five miles
home. When he arrived, there I was, sitting on the back steps, clutch-
ing the small American flag that went with me to every parade. I was
crying.

"You forgot me!"

"Get in the car," my father ordered. "Now!"

It seems that when the family was leaving, I was way up in a tree in
the backyard.

In the summers we followed the masses to our favorite vacation spot:
Cape Cod. Each year we stayed at the Melrose Inn in Harwich Port,
a daffodil yellow, rambling wood structure in the center of town.
Surrounded by beds of thriving pink and lavender impatiens, it was a
quiet, restful place—quiet and restful, that is, until the Daggett clan
descended upon it.

There were a lot of elderly people staying at the Melrose Inn then,
and Mom says she and Dad always felt a little guilty about arriving with
their seven lively kids. Every morning the ladies sat on the veranda in
their rocking chairs, chatting and crocheting and looking out at the
peaceful goings-on of Main Street.

Then I came along, and the ladies argued to have me get up on their laps.

Mom says I entertained them with my endless chatter and nonstop charm. My hair had lightened to a warm brown (it was amazing how every day I looked more and more like my father), which made my big, dark eyes seem even larger, and when I smiled Mom says she could almost see their hearts melt.

How I relished the attention! I proclaimed them all my "adopted grandmothers." Mom also says in later years that she's often thought of those friendly, patient women, and wondered what they would have thought if they'd known they had been holding a future Olympian.

It was also at the Cape that I learned there probably was no future for me as an Olympian. My sisters Susan and Sharon had become interested in gymnastics at an early age, mostly tumbling, doing splits and that sort of thing. There was a place near Harwich Port that featured in-ground trampolines, and one afternoon my parents took us there.

Susan and Sharon were—well, they were such *show-offs*, doing all kinds of neat bounces and flips.

"If they can do it, I can do it," I said to myself. They were *girls*. How hard could it be?

Not knowing anything about gymnastics, I watched them for a few minutes, then got on the trampoline. I bounced a few times, getting higher and faster with each bounce.

"This is great!" I shouted. "I'm going to do a somersault!"

Before anyone could shout back "*No!*" I bounced again, tucking myself into position and doing a perfect somersault in the air. Only I didn't know what to do next. I landed head first into the springs, getting my neck stuck, and causing my parents to scream.

So much for gymnastics.

When I was in the third grade we moved to the "big house," as we called it, set on a quiet street where the sidewalks are thick with sugar maples and red oak trees. The neighborhood had many large, older, colonial homes, perfect for raising a family. For my father, a high school biology teacher, it was even more ideal, for the backyard was large enough for a greenhouse for his future botanical "putterings"; for us kids, there was a swimming pool; and, most important to us, there were lots and lots of trees. Really big trees.

I ended up getting the short end of the stick the day we moved. While I was checking out the endless possibilities for escapades in the huge backyard, the other kids were staking claims on bedrooms.

Michael, the oldest, picked a small room on the first floor. Next came Susan, who took a room with my sister Sharon, the fourth child. Then Daniel and David, the twins, claimed a big, sunny bedroom, and the baby, Sheila, had a small room. My parents took the other room. There was no bedroom left for me to call my own.

First I figured, okay, I'll be in Michael's room.

But that was too small and after a few weeks, I decided I needed more space.

I moved into Daniel and David's room, but by then that room was theirs. I felt like a visitor. So I camped out in a tiny sewing room. Tiny wasn't the word for it. The room was so small that once we put in a twin bed, the door couldn't be opened unless I stood on the bed. I was small for my age, but the sewing room seemed even smaller.

So I moved up to the attic.

But that summer was steamy and hot, and the attic quickly turned into a sauna.

I packed my belongings again and headed for the cellar, which finally became "my room."

It wasn't exactly glamorous, but it was all mine! What I didn't know then was how this bedroom shuffling would help me in my later years "on the road." It conditioned me so I could sleep almost anywhere!

My father, John Daggett, was stern, and he continually impressed on his children the need to achieve. At an early age he had lost his own father and subsequently a sense of emotional and financial security.

Now he was determined to have his children enjoy all the things he had missed.

Dad kept us busy. Real busy. When we moved to the big house, having a built-in swimming pool was important to him. But he felt that having things was not enough—if you had them you had to use them.

That first summer in the big house all of us kids had to swim no less than ten laps each day the sun was shining, and sometimes even when it wasn't. Along with the swimming came the endless sports. Tennis and baseball during the warm months; skiing, hockey and skating during the winter.

And, of course, there was school. Starting at a young age each Daggett child was disciplined to study and to learn. Poor grades simply were not tolerated. With a father who was a teacher and an uncle who was the high school principal, getting a good education was a high priority. So was another positive attitude—family unity.

My father was really big on what he called "family projects," and I say that with a small groan. We were always doing something, always working to make things a little better, a little more out of the ordinary.

Take the Daggett skating rink, for example. Behind the house our yard sloped down into a woodsy area, where a fresh spring-fed brook trickled by. On Saturdays every fall, while the other neighborhood kids were playing or watching TV, the Daggett kids were working, damning the brook to flood the area, assuring a perfect skating rink come winter.

We couldn't just have a normal skating rink. Ours had to be flawless. It had to be the best.

The sloping backyard also provided the ideal place for a toboggan run—but, again, we could never just have an ordinary toboggan run. Dad had us build a wooden ramp at the top of the hill so we could get more speed going down. Then we flooded the course every day during the winter to make it icy and fast.

It was, by far, the best toboggan run in the neighborhood, but not without a lot of work.

That's how my father was, though—he taught us all that with a little extra work we could excel at everything, even if it was only a toboggan run.

Dad drove himself to excel as well. In addition to teaching school, he gave private lessons almost every evening, and he started a musical instrument business to serve the public school bands.

With seven children, he was always looking for ways to earn money, and he became a bit of an entrepreneur. I think he felt he needed to be in order to give his kids the kind of life he had missed.

One family project was to set the scene for other money-raising endeavors: with every member of the family taking part, we constructed Dad's long-awaited greenhouse behind the garage. We put it to use immediately.

Of Irish descent and living in an area inhabited by a large Irish population, Dad decided there was money in shamrocks. He purchased two-inch pots, some green-and-silver foil and hundreds of shamrock seeds. The plants flourished and the Daggett assembly line was put into place.

From twelve-year-old Michael to two-year-old Sheila, and every Daggett kid in between, the entire family began mixing soil, planting cuttings and wrapping each pot with the colorful foil. Everyone had a job, and everyone worked to create the perfect plant.

As St. Patrick's Day approached, we were ready. Mom dressed all seven children in green-and-white-striped vests with green bow ties and hats, and we began making the rounds of the parking lots. In one hand we even carried a plastic shillelagh.

It's really funny now to think about how we must have looked, but it was real embarrassing at the time. Here we were, seven kids looking like poor excuses for leprechauns, peddling our shamrocks for a dollar a plant. From grocery stores to street corners, we went in groups of two or three, all over town. We even went door-to-door in residential areas.

Every so often a potential customer asked, "What organization is this for? The Boys and Girls Club? The Rotary? The Kiwanis?"

"Oh, it's for the Daggett family," I'd answer.

But Susan didn't think that was good enough. "The money is for us. We've worked very hard to make these," she'd add emphatically, and, most often, locked up the sale.

Whether from our innocence or our determination, the shamrocks sold. We made what seemed like a small fortune.

The concept was so effective, in fact, that the following year we not only sold our shamrocks on the streets but placed them on consignment in several shopping centers and wholesaled them to grocery and discount stores. What had started as a way to make a little extra money had turned into a profitable business.

With my discovery that people would actually pay for something you had if they were convinced they wanted it, I decided to strike out on an entrepreneurial venture of my own. With Daniel, David and Sheila in hand, I went door-to-door in the neighborhood. I walked up to a front door and rang the bell.

"Do you want to hear a song?" I asked innocently when the door was answered.

Almost always the person would say "Of course!" probably instantly charmed, and certainly unsuspecting.

I led the group in a silly grade school rendition, and when we were finished, the neighbor usually clapped his hands and said "Thank you."

"We're glad you enjoyed it," I said, with a straight face and all the best intentions. "Now that will be twenty-five cents, please."

If the neighbor wasn't willing to pay up, we settled for cookies, then moved on to the next door.

My mother was mortified when she found out what I'd been doing. It's hard for me to believe I actually did it, too. I've always felt I was so shy. But, shy or not, somehow, when it came to performing, I seemed to be in my element, which, inevitably, led me back to gymnastics.

With Susan and Sharon as my "teachers," we worked up an attempt at a routine.

One night we went into the family room determined to entertain our father.

"One—two—three!" Susan cried, and the three of us stood on our heads. It was my first real taste of teamwork.

"What do you think, Dad?" we cried. "You could put us on TV! We could be on 'The Ed Sullivan Show'!"

My father looked up from his newspaper at the trio of wobbly head-standers.

"Okay, you can stand on your heads," he said. "Try standing on your hands instead. When you can do that, maybe we'll put you on TV."

He was only making conversation, of course. But apparently the challenge stuck in my nine-year-old mind.

That fall Sharon enrolled in a gymnastics class. I spent most of my free time playing tennis and baseball, logging in countless miles on my bicycle going to and from the local park.

One evening my brothers and sisters were all busy or out some-where. I was hanging around the kitchen, watching my mother bake, getting underfoot. It was time for her to pick up Sharon from her gymnastics class.

"Why don't you come with me to get her?" she suggested, so I went along for the ride.

When we arrived, I walked into the gym. I glanced quickly around. Then I stopped dead.

I saw one guy hanging on a bar about ten feet off the ground. He started swinging in huge circles, picking up speed, going faster and faster every time. He let go of the bar, went flying about fifteen feet in the air, did a complete back flip and landed—right on his feet.

I turned to the other end of the gym and saw another guy, sprinting down a runway, running as fast as he could. He hit a board, went flying over some kind of long, fat table—and landed on his feet, too.

I couldn't believe this was actually a *sport* . . . where I could mess around like this and not get in trouble for doing it!

Needless to say, the next week I enrolled in a gymnastics class. And the dream had begun.

2

It was not a formal sport sanctioned by the public school system, but Bill Jones, a popular coach at West Springfield High School, saw a growing interest in the gymnastics program he had started at the high school level. Now he wanted more kids in town to have the opportunity to enjoy the sport.

Coach Jones had come to West Springfield ten years earlier, in 1961. He was hired to be the assistant football coach and head track coach. He is a likable, motivating man, quick with a smile and a warm hello. He also has another feature virtually unheard of at that time in West Springfield—he is black. Coming to a town that had only one or two black families in the early sixties might have been difficult for someone else, but not for Bill Jones. In fact, the issue simply never came up.

That, perhaps, is because of the kind of man he is: always wanting to help the kids, always there when they needed extra help in training, or when they just needed someone to talk to. And always looking to find extra ways for the kids to have a healthy, good time.

It was with this purpose that Bill Jones convinced the town's park and recreation administration to develop the gymnastics program, and it was through his enthusiasm for the sport and dedication to the kids that I developed my interest.

In the beginning I attended the classes, held twice a week, but as fall turned into winter, I once again took up my favorite sport: skiing.

I was actually a much better skier than a gymnast. I loved the speed, and the control that the individual has over the results. I was always so competitive in sports. In fact, I was competitive at everything, whether it mattered or not—playing checkers, cards, or any game, I had to win!

If I didn't win, I wanted to keep playing until I did!

When I lost, I always figured it was the "other guy's" fault. But with skiing, and with gymnastics, there was no one to blame if I wasn't perfect—it was all up to me. I liked that. I liked the fact that if I kept practicing, I'd keep getting better. I also knew that if I didn't, I wouldn't. Instead of competing with others, I was competing with myself. I guess that's when my compulsion with self-discipline really began.

Living in New England, skiing was easily accessible to me through-out the winter months. But Bill Jones had sparked my enthusiasm enough so that in between skiing, I kept returning for the gymnastics classes.

By the end of the fourth grade, right after I turned ten, I eagerly awaited summer. At last, there would be more time to swing from the high bar and fly through the air! But this was also a special summer, because it was 1972 and, for the first time in memory, I watched the Olympic Games on television.

I remember those opening ceremonies as though they happened yesterday. Through the excitement of the crowd, and the pomp and circumstance surrounding the athletes, one thing stuck in my mind— the Olympic theme song.

Bom, ba-bom, ba-bom, bom, bom, bom-bom, dat-dat . . . It was hypnotic to me.

Each night during the games, after turning off the TV and going to bed, I lay there, hearing that song replaying over and over in my thoughts.

Each day I was glued to the set, and when it was time for the Men's Gymnastics competition, I was hooked. There were men with strange-sounding names like Sawao Kato, Viktor Klimenko and Akinori Nakayama. They were on the apparatus I was only just becoming familiar with—performing moves that had me awestruck: iron crosses on the rings, somersaults in the air.

"How can they do those things?" I wondered. And even at that young age I realized I wanted to learn everything possible. I wanted to be a gymnast.

But it was not yet time for me to dedicate myself solely to gymnastics. In addition to academics, sports and "family projects," being well-rounded and versatile was also strongly stressed in the Daggett household.

The musical instrument business, like everything else, was a family affair, and all the children—including me—had his or her share of "chores." From cleaning and refurbishing the instruments and cases during the busy fall rental season, to replacing reeds and handling the billing, everyone was involved. It was these endeavors that paid for all the "extras"—like family ski trips and gymnastics classes.

But sometimes I resented the musical instrument business, a resentment which perhaps started as early as the fifth grade.

I had been invited to a Halloween party—in fact, it was my first "boy-girl" party. I was both excited and nervous. I was so small for my age that I always felt like the kids my own age were actually older than I was, and I tried to keep up with them. I wanted to be excited about the party, but the truth is, I was scared.

Then my father decided to make me a special costume—one that none of the other kids would have, one that would outshine all others at the party.

I wanted to go as Batman.

But Dad had other plans, and before I knew what had happened, I was dressed in a white-sheeted toga, complete with a crown of ivy which my father had gathered from the front lawn and braided into a lavish crown.

"Who am I supposed to be?" I cried.

"Nero," my father answered proudly.

"Who's Nero?" I asked. God, I was only ten. I had no idea who he was. "I don't want to be Nero. I never heard of him."

But I went to the party, my costume completed with the unbelievable addition of an authentic, four-hundred-dollar violin.

My mother drove me there and I cried all the way.

"Who's Nero?" I kept asking her.

When she tried to explain, I tuned it out. Here I was going to my first boy-girl party as some guy in a dress with a four-hundred-dollar violin. I wanted to break it over the head of the first kid who made fun of me.

But that's how things were when I was a kid. You could never just do something in a conventional way. We had to take that extra step, be a little bit better or a little bit more involved. Sometimes, as with the Nero costume, it was pretty intense. Here was my father trying so hard to have me outfitted in the perfect costume, when all I really wanted was a black cape and mask.

With the musical instrument business, coupled with his desire for all his kids to achieve, Dad decided we should all play an instrument.

I hated it. Maybe going to that party with the four-hundred-dollar violin is what turned me off. Anyway, I figured that if I had to play an instrument, it might as well be the drums. They seemed more "macho" than a clarinet . . . and I certainly wanted no part of the violin.

I joined the band in the sixth grade, and, because my heart simply wasn't in it, I was a terrible drummer.

There was this one kid, David Small. Man, he was a great drummer. He practiced all the time and he was fantastic. He stood on the end, closest to our conductor, Mr. DiGiore. There were four of us playing the drums, and I figured out a way to fake playing and let David do all the work. I thought it was neat, and I showed it to the other kids. Funny thing is, it worked. Mr. DiGiore thought he had a great drum section, and my father was so proud of my musical talent.

Everything was going fine until one day we had a concert to do and

David was home sick. It was awful. It was the first time I tried to bluff my way through anything and I failed miserably. It was so embarrassing that it taught me a grave lesson about faking your way through life.

I never played the drums after that.

The family projects, however, did continue, this time with Dad's development of a botanical item he called the "poly pillow."

In the backyard greenhouse, he carefully blended a mixture of soils, minerals and vermiculite, then inserted the blend into a small plastic pouch. Into the pouch he planted a cutting from one of several types of plants. The cuttings grew into beautiful plants.

It wasn't long before the Daggett team of "Lucky 7 + 2" (the seven children plus my parents) were "manufacturing" hundreds of poly pillows a week on our well-planned assembly line.

Hours after school and on weekends were devoted to the poly pillows. Again, everyone was involved: laboring over the soil compositions, melting the resin to create the ideal "pillow," searching for the perfect cuttings, suffering from cramped fingers. As the demand increased, so did production.

I don't think any of us kids liked working on those things, but by then we were used to our projects. They had become a fact of life, even if we didn't totally understand the real reason Dad insisted on doing them—that he was doing them for us.

The summer of 1974, before I entered junior high, I went to my first gymnastics camp—the United States Gymnastics Training Center—at nearby Mount Hermon School in Northfield, Massachusetts.

At that point gymnastics was still something I was doing for fun, but my father had taught me that I should be serious about everything, whether it was fun or work. "The more you put into something, the more you get out of it" was his basic philosophy. About this time I started applying that way of thinking to gymnastics, too.

Aside from wanting to learn more about the sport, I was really excited about going away from home for the first time. Life was finally starting to make more sense: all the tedious, time-consuming things we had done, from selling shamrocks to cleaning instruments to making those blasted poly pillows, were enabling my parents to have the extra money to send me to camp.

That first year I went for a two-week session.

At night I went out to a big field and lay on my back looking up at the stars. The air is so clear up there, and the stars are so bright. I remember thinking how fantastic it would be if I could make it to the Olympics someday. I replayed that Olympic theme over and over in my head. The stillness of the night made my dream more vivid, and I was lulled to sleep under the stars by the music in my mind.

But although I was maturing emotionally, physically I simply did not grow. Later that summer, concerned that my slight size indicated a physiological problem, my parents took me to a pediatrician. None of my brothers or sisters was tall, but I was even smaller. At twelve years, I looked more like seven or eight.

The doctor ran some routine tests and found nothing wrong.

Once a physical problem was ruled out, he told my parents about a new drug on the market. He said its primary benefit was that it increased size and accelerated growth. But it was very expensive! There was just no way my parents could afford it. This kind of drug wouldn't have been covered under their medical insurance, and the cost was simply prohibitive.

They left the doctor's office feeling inadequate as parents because they couldn't afford the one thing that could help their child grow and be the same size as other kids his age. They were despondent, and they were feeling guilty. But looking back, we all know that what they thought was such a bleak day actually happened for the best reason.

The drug the doctor was ready to prescribe for me was a steroid. What wasn't known then was that though it would, indeed, have increased my size, it could also have had dangerous side effects which might have shortened my career and ruined my life. It turned out to be one time we are all grateful there wasn't enough money.

But though I was substantially smaller than my friends, it never held me back.

"You just have to compensate for your size," my dad told me. "You will have to work a little harder to prove you're just as good as everyone else. That is something you can control. You can do it."

That's what I did. By the time I was in the eighth grade, my love for gymnastics was full-fledged. Here was a sport at which I excelled, where my lithe, small size actually worked to my benefit, and where I could combine my innate love of performing with my desire to be the best that I could be.

With Coach Jones at my side, I threw myself into the sport I was beginning to love. The commitment and drive I was developing, however, were not confined to the supervised workouts.

I was always a restless sleeper. When I was very young, I developed a habit of banging my head against the wall behind my bed. It was very frightening for my folks, but the doctor assured them it was merely a way I had of expelling my excess energy. They often wondered if the doctor would have been so quick to disregard this if it had been one of *his* kids waking up the entire household in the middle of the night!

Once I got into gymnastics, I developed another terrifying nighttime habit: I started talking and walking in my sleep . . . and I started doing gymnastics.

One evening my mom was watching TV in the family room in the cellar with Susan and Sharon. I had gone to bed in Michael's room off the upstairs living room. From the living room down to the family room there were three steps and a landing, then the stairs continued off to the right. All was quiet, except for the low voices from the television set.

Suddenly, there was a burst of commotion on the stairs. Mom and the girls looked up just in time to see me complete a back flip down the steps.

Startled, Mom jumped up and did exactly what she'd read you shouldn't do when someone is sleepwalking: she started yelling.

"What on earth are you doing, Timothy? Don't you know you could have broken your neck?"

I opened my eyes in disbelief.

"What happened?" I asked innocently.

To this day I have no recollection of that performance.

Another time, Susan had a friend sleeping over, and in the middle of the night, I burst through the bedroom door and did a series of cartwheels into the room. The poor girl who was staying over was terrified, but was even more surprised when Susan nonchalantly said, "Wake up, Timmy. Go back to bed." Susan then looked at her friend, shrugged her shoulders and went back to sleep.

I obediently went back to bed.

For Christmas that year, one of my gifts was a gym bar. It was great! It was a simple, adjustable stainless steel pole with a suction cup on each end and it fit perfectly in any and every doorway in the house. I'd set it at midheight for doing somersaults, and higher for chin-ups. Unfortunately, sometimes I forgot to take it out of the doorway.

"*Timothy!*" became a common cry throughout the household as one of my brothers or sisters went around a corner too fast and slammed a stomach or forehead into the bar.

Finally the *"Once-more-and-it's-in-the-trash!"* threat from my parents gave me the message.

Between my love for practicing and my experience at summer camp, I had advanced so quickly that there was no one on the junior high level I could learn from—they were learning from me. Coach Jones felt I needed a challenge that could be provided only by older, more experienced boys, and it wasn't long before I began working out with the high school team. Soon I was doing back flips and giant swings superior even to those of the high school boys.

Coach says it was great for him, too, because I was the first kid he had coached who was so determined to keep on getting better. At that point, neither of us had any idea how determined I was.

Along with my commitment came the inevitable sacrifices.

It was early 1976, the year of our nation's Bicentennial. As part of the celebration, the townspeople planned a gala pageant, and I looked forward to participating in it. My natural ability for athletics plus my love of performing had led me in what I thought was an unlikely direction—dancing.

I always thought dancing was for girls. At thirteen, none of the guys I hung out with wanted to admit we might just enjoy dancing. Sure, we all loved music, but dancing . . . well, that was something you did only when you were messing around at home.

But, as with most eighth graders, my group of friends did, in fact, include a few girls. And the father of one of the girls was a dance instructor at a local college. With the impending bicentennial pageant, he decided we should get involved. He started off determined to get us to like dancing, so he taught us the "fun" dances like the jitterbug, the twist and the "mashed potato." It worked. And, if nothing else, it helped me burn off energy!

Then we were approached to take part in the pageant.

"No way," we all said at first, but that soon turned into "Why not?" and before we knew it, we were rehearsing like mad.

The pageant centered around skits of events throughout American history. Between the skits, we were to demonstrate the dance of each appropriate era, complete with period costumes.

We practiced for weeks: the waltz, the minuet, you name it. It wasn't long before we actually got excited about it. But on the day of our final costume fitting, I received bad news: there was a gymnastics meet scheduled for the same night as the pageant.

Although disappointed and feeling as though I was letting down my friends, I knew my priority.

I went to the director and explained the situation. She was so angry with me she never said a word. It was hard for me to drop out of the pageant and harder when I knew I would have to get up the courage to tell her. But she didn't seem to care about my feelings, even though I was just a kid. She brushed me off with a disgusted look. That's when I learned that not everyone would appreciate my commitment to gymnastics.

At the end of that school year, I learned another important lesson: humility.

Though I had worked out and competed with the high school team, recognition for my performance was to be limited.

"Everyone thought it was so cute when the team came out onto the floor, and here came little Timmy trailing behind them," my mother says.

But when the year was over, the mothers of the high school boys decided to raise money for team jackets—each to be lettered with the boy's name and high school. There apparently was some discussion among them about it, but in the end they agreed not to give me a jacket. Their feeling was that I had plenty of time to earn one.

At first my mother was angry over the decision, but later came to understand their thinking.

"I thought about how I would feel if this little kid, cute and capricious though he was, kept performing better than my kid, kept 'stealing the show' because he was so noticeable," she says. "I also realized they probably felt Timmy was too young to be so honored. Finally their decision made some sense to me, and I put aside my anger."

But, then, as a mother, she admits she remained a little hurt. She was worried that I might never have another chance to earn a high school gymnastics jacket.

3

That summer was filled with gymnastics for me. As each day passed, my dream became clearer and my goal more reachable. I put away my baseball mitt and tennis racket and focused all my energy on gymnastics.

Coach Bill Jones encouraged my enthusiasm, and he helped set up a "mini" camp in our backyard.

For four hours each morning, a few of my friends and I worked out under the guidance of Coach Jones. With a trampoline, parallel bars, high bar, pommel horse and tumbling mats, our group of fourteen-year-olds turned the quiet neighborhood into a training ground.

Why would a coach give up his summer to volunteer to help us out? He says it's because he wanted to have a great team! But I suspect it was just one more indication of his dedication to us kids.

Afternoons we rode our bikes several miles to a private gym club, where we spent the rest of the day working on what we had done that morning.

And, once again, it was an Olympic year.

Glued to the television set on the sultry July nights, I religiously followed every broadcast moment. While Romania's Nadia Comaneci dazzled the gymnastics world for women, to me the American men seemed shadowed in mediocrity. When the Games were over, the Men's Team medals went to Japan, the Soviet Union and East Germany; only one American, Peter Kormann, received a medal—a bronze for his floor exercise performance. With his exceptional routine, Peter became my first true hero.

Watching the United States being virtually blown away was very upsetting. I couldn't believe how much better the other countries were. I kept wondering what they were doing differently. What made them great? And, why not us? I felt like I was the one who had been defeated.

The day after the final Men's Gymnastics competition, I worked harder than ever.

Later in the summer I returned to the U.S. Gymnastics Training Center in Northfield. That year I did better, and at the end of the summer I won the camp honors for the hardest worker and the most improved gymnast.

During each session awards were given for those categories. I knew that after summer was over, the camp directors selected seven kids from among the winners to receive a free trip to Florida. I didn't think much about the possibility of winning, though. I was anxious to get home and start training again with the high school team.

When my freshman year began, however, I got a little sidetracked.

As committed to gymnastics as I was, some of my friends were developing other interests. One of them was soccer.

"Come on, Timmy," they prodded. "Try out for soccer with us!"

Using the excuse that the official gymnastics season wouldn't start until after soccer was over, and bending to peer pressure, I tried out for the team. The day after the tryouts, I raced to the gym with my friends to check the bulletin board where the team would be posted. The sheet was there and we all huddled together, searching for our names, each letting out a squeal of joy when one was found. But the name Tim Daggett did not appear on the roster.

At first I couldn't believe my eyes. I mean, me, not making a team? I don't care if it was soccer or tiddlywinks, it was unthinkable that I didn't make a team.

But there was no mistake. I had been cut from the team.

That night I went home and sulked. Aside from this being a huge embarrassment, it was humiliating.

"You must not have tried hard enough," was my father's only comment.

I thought about that. He was right. I didn't try hard enough. And the more I thought about it, I realized how out of character that was for me—not to try as hard as I could to get what I wanted. But then I knew why I hadn't tried. It was because I never really did want to make it. I wanted to spend all my free time doing gymnastics. Once I accepted that, I discovered I was almost relieved I hadn't made the team.

The next day, I went looking for Coach Jones.

"I want to work out year-round," I said to him. "And I want to start now."

Because the gymnastics season hadn't yet started, the equipment was stored in a back room. Breaking all the rules and chancing the wrath of school administrators, Coach and I pushed aside piles of mats and shoved as much of the equipment as possible against the walls of the twelve-by-eighteen-foot room. That left barely enough space for me to practice on the pommel horse.

We both had wanted to do it right, but the administrators went by the book. And according to the book, gymnastics season didn't start until November. At times Coach said he hoped we'd get caught, so he could present his case, which was, quite simply, that he had a "dedicated kid who would do anything to practice his sport. A kid who wasn't about to let an obstacle like unavailable equipment stand in his way." Boy, he sure hit the nail on the head.

We knew we were taking chances, but I didn't care. Looking back, I certainly wouldn't recommend that anyone else do it the way I did. But at the time, that just didn't matter.

A few days later Dad picked me up after school. As we pulled out onto Elm Street he handed me an envelope.

"I thought you might want to see this right away," he said.

The return address was the U.S. Gymnastics Training Center. I tore into the envelope and pulled out a letter.

"Congratulations! We are pleased to inform you . . ." the letter began. It went on to say that I had been chosen as one of the seven gymnasts to go to Florida.

I'll never forget that feeling. Winning the trip was the first type of real recognition I'd received in gymnastics and I was on top of the world. The trip itself was pretty wild. We went in October for a week. Seven gymnasts plus our chaperone packed into an old motor home wasn't exactly a vacation paradise, but it was the most exciting thing that had ever happened to me. We went to Disney World, Sea World, Busch Gardens—all the great places. I especially loved Sea World. Little did I know that eight years later I would once again be at Sea World—this time in San Diego—not as a visitor but as an Olympic gold medalist, performing in a gymnastics exhibition along with the U.S. Women's gold medalist Julianne McNamara.

Encouraged by winning the trip, I returned home and began practicing again with a vengeance.

The following February, while only a freshman, I led the high school team to win the Western Massachusetts Championships and began being noticed throughout the small gymnastics community in the area. Coach Jones always said it wasn't just the fact that I did well that mattered, but it was the way I did it. He said I attacked the apparatus without fear or hesitation; I said I was only doing what came naturally!

It was about this time that my parents let me put up a set of rings in the attic. (At least up there, they were out of everyone's way!) Night after night I climbed into the attic and dangled from the rafters, practicing iron crosses and other basic skills. It wasn't an ideal situation, but I was getting used to that, and at least it gave me a chance to do *something*. To this day, the rings still hang there.

After the Western Massachusetts Championships, Coach Jones began looking around. He knew it wasn't wise for me to continue training in the supply room during the off-season. It was not only against the rules, but it was too restrictive for me. He knew I needed a gym.

So Coach started making phone calls. That spring, after the high school season officially ended and the apparatus was once again locked away, I started working out at one of the area colleges.

Coach also knew my frustrations were increasing. He knew I needed a challenge; I needed to be able to learn from watching others. He could tell me what to do, but at fifty years of age, he couldn't jump up on the high bar, the rings or the parallel bar and show me, much as he wanted to.

I have to admit I was more than a little nervous the first time I walked into the college gym. I don't know what I expected, but I know I wasn't sure how the students would react to me. Aside from the fact that I wasn't quite fifteen, I was still pretty small for my age. All the apparatus was being used, so I timidly warmed up and headed for the tumbling mats.

With Coach Jones beside me, I broke into the best floor routine I was capable of doing. I guess I was trying to prove something to these college guys. It wasn't long before I realized that proving things to myself was more important.

As it turned out, there was no need for feeling any intimidation. The college team quickly made friends with me: I guess it was easy for them to see my commitment to the sport.

Gymnastics was now a way of life. Each day I worked at getting stronger, getting better. By the time I entered my sophomore year, the local press had me earmarked for success.

I could never have gotten as far as I did without my incredible support system. Whether it was my parents driving me to and from workout, or my older brother spending his only weekend off to come and watch me compete, I always had the strongest support from my family.

But there were times when my parents questioned whether they were doing the right thing by allowing me to become so immersed in gymnastics.

This doubt came through loud and clear to my mom at one event in particular. It was a high school meet, and the outcome was to determine which school would go on to the Western Massachusetts Championships.

I had a problem with some bone chips in my wrist. The doctor had pushed the chips into place, and fitted me with a cast to hold them securely. Mom wasn't too happy that I was going to compete with a cast on, but the doctor said I would be fine.

She didn't question him. At least, not until she was sitting in the high school bleachers.

Just before I was to perform on floor exercise, another boy was doing his routine. He misjudged his landing and went crashing onto the floor. To this day I don't know what happened to him, but I know they took him out on a stretcher and put him in an ambulance.

Mom says she looked over and saw me about to mount the bar, cast and all. She wanted to start screaming "No! Timothy, get down!" She wanted to pull me out of the gym and never let me go back. She thought she had to be out of her mind to let me perform with a cast on.

She doesn't know what kept her from making me stop. She says she only saw the determination and concentration on my face as I mentally prepared for my routine. She also says she thinks that's when she realized there was nothing she would be able to do to stop me from going after my dream. I walked up to the floor mat and began. I did fine.

My support system included, of course, Coach Jones. He was always finding places for me to work out, always looking for new ways to keep me going a step further. When one college changed its rules, which meant I could no longer train there, Coach found another college willing to have me work out with its team.

It didn't matter that the school was twenty-five miles from West Springfield: before I had my driver's license, Coach himself drove me.

The guys at that school were just as great as the other college guys had been. They were aware of my problem of needing a place to work out, and they were only too willing to help.

So willing, in fact, that they risked getting into trouble themselves.

During vacations or on holidays the gym was locked. In order that I could still work out though they wouldn't be around, the guys showed me how I could pry open the gym doors with the aid of a coat hanger. We hid the coat hanger outside the gym, ready for my arrival day or night. I asked one of my parents to drive me to the school, usually taking one or two of my brothers so I'd have someone to spot for me. ("Spotting" is one of the major responsibilities of a coach. When you're flying in the air and about to land on your head or other inappropriate body part, the coach must do whatever it takes to make sure you land properly and don't get hurt. Who better to do this when a coach wasn't around than a caring brother?)

My parents, of course, had no idea what I was up to. They assumed the college team would be there, and I never told them otherwise. Maybe that was my expression of teenage rebellion!

My brothers and I pried open the huge steel doors, then I went to the electrical panel and flooded the gym with light. I cannot believe I never got caught. Even while I was doing it I knew it was stupid . . . but it was just something I wanted so badly.

To this day, there probably still is a coat hanger carefully concealed behind a fire extinguisher outside the college gym.

That year I was going to compete in the State Championships. I wanted to be ready; I wanted to be perfect. My wrists were still bothering me a little, so I went to the training room and found my first—and only—pair of wrist wraps, two eight-foot-long strips of one-inch-wide cotton.

Just before the competition began I went through the paces of winding the wrap around each wrist—one, two, three, a dozen times, checking the tension, not too tight, not too loose, but just enough to squeeze the bones and reinforce the strength. I wrapped a strip of adhesive around them, then slipped a cut-off sock over that.

With the new wrist wraps in place, I was ready to compete. I won the State Individual Championships.

The next day, my father made a call to the United States Gymnastics Federation.

"My son wants to go to the Olympics, and I want to know how he can get there," he said.

A patient, but emphatic voice replied, "How old is he?"

"Fifteen," he answered. "And he just won the Massachusetts state title."

"What team does he compete with?"

"The high school team."

"The *public* high school team?"

"Yes. West Springfield."

The man paused, then said, "Your son is the right age group to try out for the Junior National Olympic Team. But are you telling me he has no other competitive experience?"

My father thought a moment. "He has been competing with the high school team since he was in the eighth grade. And he's been going to some camps in the summer months."

Apparently the message came through loud and clear, for the man answered abruptly, "I'm afraid the boy has not received proper training to try out for the Junior Nationals. Don't waste your money or our time by sending him."

That night Dad announced to me, "You're going to try out for the Junior Nationals. The man at the USGF wasn't very encouraging, but he has never seen you perform." My father was not to be dissuaded.

4

When I boarded the plane for the Junior Nationals in Colorado Springs with Coach Jones, I was nervous. I had never flown before, and I had no idea what to expect at the trials. But I knew my big opportunity had arrived, and I knew I was good. Well, I *thought* I was good.

Upon our arrival, Coach and I reviewed the schedule. On the first day were the compulsory events. On the second day were the optional events.

"What do they mean by 'compulsories'?" I asked Coach. "And what are 'optionals'?"

"I don't know," Coach replied honestly.

That night I didn't sleep at all.

The next day we found out what was expected. "Compulsories" relate to set routines comprising specific skills on each apparatus, most of which I'd never heard of. Every competitor must perform those skills identically: it is the proper execution of them that provides a solid base for good gymnastics.

The "optionals" allow gymnasts to develop their individual routines by combining various skills at which they excel, including their own creations. While the optionals can quickly hide a gymnast's weaknesses, they can also showcase his or her strengths.

I had few strengths and many weaknesses. My performance was a disaster. I watched others perform moves I had never heard of. Kids my own age—and younger—dominated the apparatus in ways I had never dreamed. When it was my turn to compete, I was devastated. I had no idea what I was doing. But I tried. I did not do well, not at all. I simply couldn't come close to the experience of the other boys . . . boys like the Hayden twins, Jim Mikus and others.

I knew there was obviously no way I would make the team, so I used the time to another advantage: I watched, I studied and I learned.

On the way back to New England, we had a layover in Chicago. It was just after Christmas, and the airport was bustling with people, all bundled in winter wools and mohair scarfs, juggling packages and suitcases, and in a hurry.

Coach and I sat on the cold plastic chairs in the O'Hare terminal, waiting for our next flight. I sipped a cup of hot chocolate from a Styrofoam cup. I stirred it with a wooden stick, then looked at Coach.

"Man, that hurt. I really thought I was good, but I guess I'm not," I said.

Coach Jones didn't say anything. He sat quietly, allowing me to get the words out.

"But I'm going to be good, Coach," I continued. "In fact, I'm going to be great."

"Well, you sure are better than anyone else in the state."

I shook my head. "No, Coach. I'm going to be better than that. I'm going all the way. I'm going to make it to the Olympics."

It was the first time I said those words and knew I meant them. From watching the other boys I had faced the reality of the enormous task ahead of me. But I knew I had to try.

After we returned, Coach Jones met with my parents. He told them he wasn't sure I'd be able to get the right training in West Springfield. As he saw it, there were two options: either I should get another coach and private training with someone experienced in training Olympic athletes, or Coach could arrange for the two of us to go to Japan to train: me as an exchange student, Coach as an exchange teacher.

Both options proved to be out of the question. My parents simply could not afford it.

I was relieved. Even though I knew my dream, I wasn't ready to leave home. I wanted to stay in West Springfield; I wanted to keep working with Coach.

With that decision made, Coach Jones began investigating all we would need to know.

Coach always said that being a good coach doesn't just mean being able to train an athlete, but, more than that, it means being able to reach beyond your own knowledge and seek the advice and support of others with more experience. So he reached beyond his own knowledge, and we began our training with intensity.

As part of my training, I purchased a diary. Each night I recorded the exact skills practiced that day, as well as areas where I felt I needed extra work. I reviewed the entries continually, checking my progress and noting my improvement.

One Saturday afternoon, while watching ABC's "Wide World of Sports," I was captivated by one athlete who, recovering from an injury and working at a comeback, talked about something I quickly related to.

"No matter what the obstacles, I will always push ahead," he said. Then he shared with the audience a quotation that he said always inspired him:

"If you give up your dream, you'll die."

I sat motionless for a moment, absorbing the impact of the athlete's words. I went to my room, took out my training diary and opened it. On the inside front cover, I carefully lettered the athlete's quotation: IF YOU GIVE UP YOUR DREAM, YOU'LL DIE.

I sat back and reread the words, filled with a renewed sense of confidence in my determination, and a newfound peace in my purpose.

It was this quote that marked the beginning of my intensely personal and deeply meaningful ongoing search for motivational messages, a search I carry out to this day.

In my junior year I won the State Championships again, even more easily than before. I had spent the previous year doing nothing but studying and training. And when the Junior Nationals trials came once again, this time I was ready.

Before I left, my father gave me a poem to carry with me. I have kept it all these years, tucked inside my wallet:

The Man Who Thinks He Can

If you think you are beaten, you are;
If you think you dare not, you don't!
If you'd like to win, but think you can't,
It's almost a cinch you won't.

If you think you'll lose, you're lost;
For out in the world we find
Success begins with a fellow's will;
It's all in the state of mind!

If you think you're outclassed, you are;
You've got to think high to rise.
You've got to be sure of yourself
Before you can win the prize.

Life's battles don't always go
To the strongest or fastest man;
But sooner or later the man who wins
Is the man who thinks he can!

(Anonymous)

The Junior Nationals were being held at West Point that year, a blessing in that it was close enough to home so my parents were spared another costly flight.

The expenses for my training were beginning to mount up. There were endless fees, transportation and room and board—for both myself and Coach—but my parents knew this was so important to me. When it came to birthdays and Christmas, however, these costs had to be taken into consideration. While the other kids got large gifts, mine were less costly. I knew gymnastics was my real gift; I knew there was only so much money to go around, and that was my choice.

During warm-ups for the trials, I was on floor exercise. I was having a great routine, putting all my strength into it. Then on one tumbling pass I went off the mat and smacked my head on the bare floor.

I sat up and felt a strange sensation. It was almost as if something had drained out of my body. I looked up and saw Coach running toward me.

"What are you doing here, Coach?" I asked.

"What do you mean, what am I doing here?"

"Why are you at camp?"

"Camp? Tim, we're at West Point. This is the Junior Nationals."

But I looked blankly at Coach, then repeated my question.

"What are you doing here, Coach?"

A trip to the hospital emergency room revealed that I had suffered a mild concussion and a resultant case of temporary amnesia. A few hours later, I was released.

"Do you want to continue?" Coach asked me on our way back to the gym.

"Of course!" I replied. "The doctor said it was okay, and I came here to do a job. Now let's do it!"

The next day were the compulsory events. Though it was still new to me, I worked at doing my best. At the end of the day, I was in twelfth place . . . a much better showing than I had had the previous year, but still a number of points out of the tenth-place requirement to make the team. The following day—the optional events—would determine the team.

That night Coach and I went out for something to eat, then returned to our room.

Coach talked to me. "I think you'd better lie down and relax and think about the job you have to do tomorrow. Think how much this really means to you."

The next day, I was supercharged.

People who had seen me in Colorado Springs were talking—I guess they couldn't believe I was the same kid. I increased my scores tremendously, and ended up in fifth place. I had made the Junior National Team.

With this success, my small-town roots began to extend beyond West Springfield, as I started to travel with the team.

My brothers and sisters claim they actually missed having me around the house when I traveled. That's probably true, especially since I always managed to be out of town at a meet when it came time to mow the lawn, rake the leaves or shovel the snow!

"Big Mac will just have to take my place," I told them before I left for yet another meet. Big Mac was our leggy, lovable Doberman pinscher, who my sister Susan had just trained to knock over the cast-iron doorstop when he wanted to go out.

"Guess I'll have to train him to use a shovel," Susan said.

I traveled with my schoolbooks tucked under my arm, studying mostly on airplanes and in waiting rooms.

One trip in particular that I remember was my first international competition—the Cottbus Invitational in East Germany.

I was now a senior in high school, seventeen, and had finally grown to a respectable five feet six inches. My childhood spunkiness had stayed with me, and I still loved to "always be doing something."

This trait created a problem for me when the plane landed in Amsterdam for a brief layover. We had about two hours to kill, and I really wanted to see part of the city. I was traveling with Jim Mikus—another Junior National boy, who was later to become the 1984 alternate at the Olympics.

Jim and I left our carry-on bags with his coach. It was warm in Amsterdam, so I took off my leather jacket and laid it across the bags.

When we came back, everything seemed okay. We boarded the plane to East Germany.

As we taxied down the runway after landing in East Germany, we couldn't help but notice the starkness. Everything was concrete and steel. It didn't exactly look inviting. Then Jim spotted the guards at the entrance . . . they were armed with machine guns. That was the first time either of us had seen machine guns. It was pretty scary, but then, we were only seventeen, so we started laughing about it.

"Yeah, they're really tough!" Jim said. "Look at that guy over there. He couldn't shoot straight if he had to."

We got off the plane laughing. I put my jacket back on, and we headed inside to go through immigration. The starkness we had seen outside was nothing compared with the bleak interior. In single file, we were directed to a window.

There was a woman behind the window who looked like she hadn't smiled in twenty years. She had a boxlike face and wore a plain gray uniform with red epaulets. Her hair was thick and unstyled, her face devoid of makeup.

"Passport," she demanded, when it was my turn.

I reached inside my jacket to get my passport. I couldn't feel it. I felt through all the pockets. It wasn't there. My first thought was that it had fallen out on the plane. Then I did the dumbest thing I could have done.

Without thinking, I turned and ran back through the terminal. I raced through the doors onto the runway, up the stairs and back into the plane. I ran down the aisle to where Jim and I had been sitting, frantically searching between the seats and on the floor.

"Halt!" I heard from behind, as two German soldiers burst into the cabin, their machine guns aimed at me.

"I came back to find my passport," I said meekly, my heart racing. "I lost my passport."

The guards did not understand English. One took me by the arm, the other kept a gun aimed, and they escorted me off the plane.

At that point I realized I shouldn't have run back to the plane. I was scared. Suddenly those machine guns didn't look so funny. But I was even more afraid when they brought me into a tiny room and closed the door.

The guards screamed at me in German.

"I don't understand German," I pleaded.

The guards left me there, closing the door behind me. I figured they locked it, but I'm not sure. All I know is I sat perfectly still on a wooden chair.

Then another uniformed man marched into the room. He, too, screamed at me in German.

"I don't understand German," I repeated.

This went on for about an hour, with various guards coming and going, each screaming at me in German. Suddenly a man entered with a camera. He motioned for me to stand up against the wall.

"This is it," I thought. "I'm being arrested."

They took my picture and left me once again. I sat back down and stared around the gray cement walls of the cubicle, wondering if I would ever see my family again. I felt a long, long way from West Springfield.

A few moments later two men returned and thrust a card into my hand. I glanced at it. My picture had been applied.

"This is your identification while you are in this country," one man said in perfect English. He was also one of the men who had screamed at me in German. "You may go."

I couldn't believe they understood what I was saying all along. In retrospect, that fact made the incident even more frightening.

I never again left my passport carelessly lying around in my jacket pocket.

Several colleges began recruiting me during my senior year. Among them was UCLA, though I had just about decided not to go there. Their team was working with a new coach, Mako Sakamoto. It was his first year there, and prior to that the team hadn't been outstanding. I knew that in order to make it to the Olympics, I needed to be part of an outstanding team.

I began visiting the other schools.

But I made sure I was in West Springfield for the Western Massachusetts Championships.

I had a really good meet at those championships. The growing local crowd made it especially fun to perform, and, incredibly, I shattered four previously held records on the rings, vault, parallel bars and high bar. And my performance enabled the team to go on to victory.

But every day was not easy for me.

After the Western Massachusetts Championships we began training even harder for the State Championships. One night, after a particularly tough workout, I went home exhausted. I was sore, I was discouraged, and I had fallen off the pommel horse more than ever. I was having my doubts that I could make it.

But that night I was excited nonetheless, because there was going to be a gymnastics meet on television. I ran home, turned on the TV and saw that the meet was dominated by one gymnast—Peter Vidmar.

I couldn't believe how good he was. I couldn't believe he was that much better than I was. But I had a funny feeling I had seen him before. His name was familiar. Then it hit me.

It was at the National Sports Festival the year before. After warming up, I had glanced around the gym to see what the other competitors were doing. I looked toward the high bar just in time to see one gymnast try a new skill—a straddled front flip. The gymnast missed the bar and landed on his back.

"Who's that on high bar?" I asked one of the assistants.

"Peter Vidmar," was the response.

That was the last I ever thought about him. Not only did he fall, but he did it all wrong—you *never* land on your back, it's dangerous. I laughed to myself, certain that Peter Vidmar was one competitor *I'd* never have to worry about.

Now Peter was outshining every other gymnast at the meet.

The television commentator gave Peter's statistics—he was nineteen, a freshman at UCLA.

For Peter to be that much better than me and only one year older, and to have come so far in the past year—well, I started to reconsider UCLA. I knew at that moment I had to check this guy out.

I went out to UCLA and was met by the assistant coach, Mako. The first thing that hit me was the weather. I had left behind a slushy, chilly New England February, and emerged from the plane into sunshine, warmth and palm trees. All in all, not a bad way to start.

Mako took me immediately to the gym, where I saw Peter, Mitch Gaylord and the rest of the team working out. I was impressed with what I saw, but was even more impressed with the coach.

Mako did something none of the other coaches on recruiting trips had done: he talked to me, really talked to me. We sat in the lobby of the Holiday Inn on Wilshire Boulevard. Mako talked. I listened. I knew that Mako had been one of our country's leading gymnasts. I learned that Mako had spent years training in Japan with the greatest gymnasts in the world, and that, he, along with his brother, had been coaching at a private school prior to joining the UCLA staff—the same school at which Peter had received his precollege training.

Mako told me his philosophy of training.

"If you come to UCLA, Timmy, it is going to be tough. It is going to be hell."

He asked me what I expected, what my hopes and dreams were. He said that, together, we could make it happen.

"But we are not just going to recruit you, Timmy," he added. "If you want to come to UCLA, you must prove yourself to us, prove that we want you."

After only forty-eight hours in Los Angeles, I boarded a plane to return home. It was a long flight, and I did some serious soul-searching. Though I still hadn't made up my mind where to go to school, I had been leaning toward Nebraska. They had an outstanding record for producing superior gymnasts. But there was something about

Mako that really piqued my interest. But I had my doubts about UCLA, man, I had doubts.

"Why not bet on a sure thing?" I asked myself repeatedly. "Nebraska *always* wins! Why take a chance on an unproven team?" By the time the plane landed, I was more confused than before I had left.

5

When I returned home there were more urgent things to think about. The State Championships were to be held in March, and they were going to be in West Springfield.

It was expected that there would be a huge crowd, and there was. For a sport which only a few years earlier had as spectators just a few parents of the competitors sprinkled throughout the gym, there now had to be additional folding bleachers brought in. There was a charge of enthusiasm throughout the community.

Once again, we didn't disappoint the crowd.

We won the Championships. But even more important to me, the entire team performed spectacularly, and, as a team, West Springfield won an *easy* victory. It was such a credit to Coach Jones. He finally got the recognition he deserved for all his years of hard work. It was important for me—and for us—to win, but it was even more important for Coach. It was the climax of a lot of years of effort. The nicest part was that my father had been keeping the statistics throughout the meet, and he later announced that the team would have won the Championships even if I hadn't competed. That made it even more special to Coach.

Right after the Championships, my high school gymnastics career now over, I had to make up my mind about college.

There were several colleges that had shown an interest in me. I visited only six—the maximum number of recruiting trips allowed by National Collegiate Athletic Association regulations. I decided on a date, and told the coaches I would make my decision then. I told them to call at 9:00 P.M.

When that night arrived, I sat in the living room with my parents. I'll admit that I wanted them to make the decision for me. Picking a college was more than just a choice of where I could get a good education. Of course that was important—all through high school I had continued to work hard in school—but gymnastics was my life, and I wanted it to go on being my life. I had to pick the right school.

Neither of my parents would make my decision for me. I guess they knew better than to do that.

By five minutes to nine, my anxiety was unbearable. I took the phone off the hook. I paced. I talked ceaselessly for about half an hour. I was trying to work it through, trying to come up with the right direction. I was waiting for a bolt of lightning to strike me on the head and give me the answer; I was waiting for my parents to say "go here," or "go there."

When no lightning struck, and my parents kept insisting it was my decision, I finally said, "Oh, forget it. I'm sick of this. I don't care anymore."

I put the phone back on the hook and it rang. It was Mako.

"Timmy, how're you doing?" Mako asked. "So, Timmy, are you going to be a UCLA Bruin?"

I looked over at my parents and smiled. "Yeah, Mr. Mako," I said, "I'm going to be a Bruin." At that instant, I knew I had made the right choice.

I graduated with the West Springfield High School class of 1980 that June. On graduation day, I wore the purple and gold sash of the National Honor Society over my royal blue gown. My parents were proud of my athletic achievements, but they were even more proud that I had not let gymnastics interfere with my grades. But I was no fool—I knew that if my grades began to slip, the first thing my father would do is take away my gymnastics. That was something worth studying for!

Right after graduation I prepared to leave for Los Angeles to begin early training.

Saying good-bye to my family was one part of leaving home I hadn't anticipated. With the excitement of going to L.A., I had packed as though this were just another trip, albeit a lengthy one. But when we all got to the airport it was different than in the past.

God, my mother started crying.

Although I was the third child, Michael, the oldest, had chosen to remain at home and was a student at American International College in Springfield; Susan, the second-oldest, was working in the thriving family musical instrument and poly pillow businesses. I was the first to leave home.

Just before I boarded the plane I looked at my parents, my brothers and my sisters. I felt an incredible pull toward them. We were all so close, and though my father had been so strict, at times had seemed so cold, I saw that beneath it all he had developed a tightly woven group who really needed and loved each other. I picked up my bag and headed for the gate, then turned back for one last look. That's when I saw the tears in Dad's eyes.

Though the UCLA school year didn't officially start until October 1, I was able to go out to L.A. in June as part of my training for the Junior National Olympic Team. But money was such a problem, I had to start thinking about how I was going to make my way around.

The school would be paying my full expenses while I was enrolled, but I had to get through the summer. When the question of where I could live arose, Peter Vidmar's family came to the rescue.

Doris and John Vidmar lived just outside Los Angeles. Peter was the only one of their six children still living at home, and they had an abundance of room. They suggested I live with them.

It was really amazing. Here I was, this kid they didn't even know, and they were willing to put me up in their home. Being with them helped me avoid any real homesickness, because the Vidmars have a strong, close family, too.

Each day Peter and I went to the gym and spent the entire day working out. At night Peter usually went out with his girlfriend, Donna, while I dealt with the one thing that plagued me my first few weeks in L.A.: I was dead tired. My body had a terrible time adjusting—both to the grueling workouts and to the smog. Each routine I did took more energy out of me than before. I knew I would adjust, but was surprised it took so long.

It was a summer of mixed emotions for Peter: he had become one of the many victims of the U.S. Olympics boycott. But Peter is such a strong, realistic guy. If that had happened to me I think I'd have been devastated—and furious. But Peter was controlled and logical. I learned a lot from him that summer.

Being the "new kid in town" did, however, have me a little intimidated.

I wasn't just a kid from a small town in New England moving out to the fast pace of L.A.; I was a kid from a small town in New England *who had spent the better part of his life in a gym*, moving out to the fast pace of L.A. That's when I realized you have to make your own environment, wherever you are. I focused on the job ahead of me, and on my concerns about being the youngest as well as the newest. I tried not to think about the beach, the laid-back environment or the knockout blonds who were everywhere.

I was the only incoming freshman gymnast. Every day I watched the guys training, and I knew I had a long way to go to make my dream come true. But then one day, a funny thing happened.

After a workout, I left the gym and headed up Bruin Walk. This sidewalk—a UCLA landmark—connects the gym to the rest of the campus, and has seen the footsteps of many an athlete who has gone on to greatness. I was thinking about how much better the other guys were than I was, about how far I had to go. But that day I had watched

Peter fall off the pommel horse; I had seen Mitch struggle through his routine on the still rings.

Suddenly I had a revelation of sorts. I knew that Peter, Mitch and the others worked very hard. But they were no more talented or "gifted" than I was. All through my early years I had been faced with better-trained, higher-jumping or stronger guys. But did they actually end up ahead in the long run? That was the question. In junior high I had watched high school gymnasts who were much more talented than I was. In high school and certainly on the Junior National team, I had worked out with others who were much more gifted. But what had happened to them? Where were they now?

I realized then that it isn't necessarily the "naturally gifted" people who make it, but rather the ones who have a dream and are willing to pay the price to make that dream come true.

That day, on Bruin Walk, I knew I could make it, too.

Excited as I was to be in Los Angeles, I looked forward to escaping the smog. A few weeks after I arrived, I went to the Junior Nationals' training camp back east in Pennsylvania. While there I roomed with Mitch—a member of the Senior Developmental Team, future UCLA Bruin teammate and 1984 Olympian. Mitch and I had known each other only slightly, having seen each other at various meets, and having trained at the same time since my move to L.A. But it's different when you room with someone. I don't think Mitch was ready for me.

The first night at the camp, we went to the movies. *Dressed to Kill*, a thriller starring Angie Dickinson and Michael Caine, was playing.

Mitch had a hard time getting to sleep that night, with images of murder and mayhem replaying in his mind. But not me. I reserved my tension for after I had fallen asleep. Though I had long since stopped doing back flips and cartwheels in my sleep, I still talked, or rather, yelled.

In the middle of the night, just as Mitch was finally drifting off to sleep, I sat bolt upright in bed and screamed.

"Mitch, look out!"

Mitch jumped from his bed and yelled "What? Where?"

I looked at him calmly, lay back down and continued sleeping.

The truth is, I don't remember anything about it, but in the morning when Mitch told me, I wasn't surprised. However, I did figure that this guy, who was a year older than I was, would most certainly never want to room with me again.

But a few weeks after we returned to L.A., Mitch suggested that I move into the apartment he shared with three other gymnasts. It wasn't so much that Mitch was a glutton for punishment—they needed someone else to help share the rent!

As grateful as I was for the Vidmars' hospitality, it made more sense for me to move in with the guys. Their apartment was right next to the UCLA campus, and I would no longer be dependent on Peter for a ride to and from the gym.

Using most of the money I received from family graduation gifts, I paid my share of the rent through the first of October, when I would move into the dorm. That left little cash, but I put all my wiles of "financial survival" into place and went full steam ahead.

Other than the rent, I think I spent about twenty dollars the rest of that summer. I was just so afraid to spend a dime. I knew I couldn't call home for money—my family had done so much already, made so many sacrifices for me. It was time for me to do it on my own. This was my dream, not theirs.

The others who shared that cramped apartment included brothers Mark and Chris Caso and Eric Gaspard—all UCLA team members. Mitch, Mark and Eric had jobs working the hot dog stand at the UGLA rec center, and for the rest of the summer our dietary mainstay consisted of hot dogs, popcorn, potato chips, ham-and-cheese sandwiches and M&M's. Not exactly what one would consider the diet of Olympic hopefuls. But it was free.

Of course we never ate that stuff for breakfast! Knowing how important it is to eat a good breakfast, we simply devised another plan, with the help of the girls on the Women's Gymnastics Team. One of the girls had a friend who worked at a local restaurant, and each week she brought us a sackful of day-old (sometimes older) goodies such as croissants. That was breakfast. They were a little dry, but edible. We washed them down with canned juice from the hot dog stand.

The apartment had two bedrooms, which had already been claimed by the other four guys, so I slept on a rollaway bed in the living room. Once again, my sleeping situation at home had conditioned me perfectly.

Mako suggested that each day, as part of the morning workout, I make a commitment to run one mile—no matter what the weather, how I felt or whatever excuse I might think of at the time. At first it didn't seem like a very big deal. I mean, what's one mile? In fact, it seemed kind of trivial, because there was already so much other physical training—training directly related to gymnastics. But Mako made the suggestion, and he had a way of making suggestions that let you know you'd better do it!

It wasn't long before I figured out Mako's reasoning. Running that mile every day became one more chip in my own corner—one more positive thing I was doing to reinforce my determination. It wasn't that the run was going to produce a better backspring or more solid dismount, it was the *sacrifice* that was important, and the knowledge that it was one more thing I'd done that maybe the others had not. Making the commitment to run every day was simply additional preparation for the bigger commitment I had ahead of me, a commitment that would prepare me to go on, no matter what my frame of mind or what condition my body was in on any given day. With that in mind, I knew that as long as my legs could hold me up, I was going to run.

With the exception of when I was seriously injured, I did, indeed, run that mile every day during the entire four years until the Olympic Games, faithfully logging each mile in my training diary.

After morning workout, we lay in the sun, swam in one of the huge pools at the rec center, then went back to work out for the rest of the day. It was a lot of fun that summer, getting to know the guys and getting into the routine of intense training. I learned, oh, I learned so much.

One of the many things I learned was from watching Mark Caso train. About a year earlier Mark had broken his neck when he fell during a floor exercise tumbling pass. He was still rehabilitating, and though I'd had my share of minor injuries, I'd never seen anyone struggle to come back from something so serious.

Witnessing Mark's struggle, both the physical and emotional aspects of it, was a greatly motivating experience for me. I saw Mark rise above the pain, determined to regain his strength and agility. And though he didn't say much about it, I was also aware of his other pain—the pain of fear—and how he worked to conquer that fear of falling every time he flipped on the floor or let go of the high bar.

At the time I thought I was only learning the positive benefits of strong internal drive; I didn't realize I was learning coping techniques which I would later need myself.

But as much as I learned from Mark, so did Mark learn from me. For Mark, I think I brought a little of the innocence back to the sport. I was still totally fearless. Coach Jones had always told me that, unlike other gymnasts, I had an uncanny way of blasting through my routines with a vengeance, naive to the possibility that I might be injured. Mark watched my fearlessness every day, and I think it helped him regain his confidence.

It was also about this time that, seeing my daily attack of the apparatus, my UCLA teammates coined a nickname for the kid from back east—a nickname that was picked up by sportswriters and followed me throughout my career.

They called me "The Bull."

Our friendships developed as we spent day and night together. We always did things as a group. None of us had much money—me, the least of all—so for the rest of the summer we devised ways to spend our free time on a nonexistent budget.

One way we accomplished this was through our acquaintance with a sportswriter for the *UCLA Bruin*, the college newspaper. Luckily for us, he also worked as a manager for the local movie theater! I think I can still remember all the lines to *Urban Cowboy*, we saw it so often that summer. But that, too, was free!

We tried other things, too. In this never-ending quest not to spend money, Mark was a real innovator. One day he suggested we go to Magic Mountain, a nearby amusement park.

We went to one of the back gates.

"We're the UCLA Bruin Gymnastics Team, and we're here to give a gymnastics exhibition," Mark informed the guard.

"Nobody told me I should let you guys in," the guard replied gruffly.

"We'll prove it. Just watch," Mark said. Then, right there in the parking lot, he led us in a series of handstands and back flips.

The guard made a call. Then he frowned.

"Sorry, boys," he said.

We proceeded to another gate, where we repeated the same performance. After several gates, several guards and no luck, we finally gave up.

It was a little embarrassing, but it was fun. Until the end, Mark really believed they would let us in.

With the end of summer came the time for me to move into the dorm. Because I was the only freshman gymnast, I would not be rooming with another gymnast. It was disappointing, but I didn't realize how disappointing until I met my roommate.

He was everything I wasn't. He was rich, he was spoiled, and he was totally L.A. At night I would lie in bed and try to bring my dream into focus—to hear the Olympic theme song, to hear the visionary voice saying "next up for the United States, on pommel horse, Tim Daggett." I was continually interrupted by this roommate, who believed that nighttime was party time. It was distracting, but only gave me more energy during the day. I knew for the time being I had to stay in the dorm, so I took out my frustrations the same way I always had—the only way I knew how—by working harder in the gym.

6

he workouts were becoming structured now, definitive with purpose and designed to make us struggle. I loved it. But suddenly something started to go wrong with my right ankle. Every time I bailed through the bottom on the high bar or did a flyaway dismount off the rings, my ankle would come out of joint. Mako and I both knew I would need surgery to repair the problem, and the sooner the better. If I could get the surgery behind me there was a strong possibility I would still be able to compete by the first of the year.

To say the least, I was disappointed. For years I had worked toward doing gymnastics on the college level. Now, that goal was in jeopardy. And worse than that, though dislocating an ankle, I know, doesn't seem to be a very big deal, to a gymnast it can end a career.

On October 4, 1980, the surgery was performed. That's when the doubters came out of the woodwork.

"Tim Daggett? Naw, he'll never make it. He doesn't have what it takes," were the rumblings throughout much of the gymnastics community.

I'd like to say that I mustered up all the psychological strength I could find and said to myself, "I'll show them!" But the truth is, I thought it was kind of amusing. Whether I was just too innocent to know better, or too stubborn to believe them, the thought simply never crossed my mind that I would not make it back. Maybe that happened to others, but not to me. God knows why I felt that way, because the statistics said otherwise.

So there I was, a freshman at UCLA, a gymnast on crutches less than one week after the school year began. I started thinking about what things I could control, and what things I couldn't.

Well, there wasn't much I could do about my foot in the cast. Scratch that.

I couldn't do much, either, to speed up the healing process and shorten the eight to ten weeks in the cast that the doctors anticipated. Scratch that.

And I certainly couldn't work out with my usual gusto—the simple fact was that a person on crutches doesn't do very well at sticking flyaway dismounts. Hmm.

There had to be something in this situation I could control. There had to be some way I could take advantage of this, some aspect which I could use to turn all the negatives into a positive.

Then one day it hit me. I was hobbling across campus, late for class, when I became aware of the way walking "normally" on crutches is tough on the underarms. After all, crutches have rubber padding be- cause when most people walk with crutches—though they use their arms somewhat—the bulk of their weight usually ends up resting on their underarms. Not for me. Not if I was going to find a way to use this to my advantage.

"That's it!" I actually said aloud. I had found my solution.

Pommel horse had become my favorite event, but until now I was lacking sufficient upper body strength to be as good on it as I wanted. If I could figure out a way to manipulate the crutches without letting my underarms touch the rubber pads, I would be stressing-out and stretching out my arm and chest muscles continuously, with every step. It would be sort of like doing nonstop push-ups, and was bound to increase my upper body strength.

I tried it, and I felt the gratifying tension in those muscles. It worked!

So, I made another one of those famous commitments to myself: as long as I was on those crutches I would under no circumstances allow my upper body to relax so that my underarms would touch the rubber padding.

With each step, I pushed myself harder to pick up more speed.

"Go. Go. Don't let it touch," I commanded myself over and over as I hobbled down the sidewalk. On the half-mile walk from my dorm to my class I got some pretty strange looks, and I guess I looked a little ridiculous. But I knew what I was doing, and I knew why.

It certainly would have been easier if I'd just used the crutches in a normal manner, and, God knows, I'd have made it to my classes a lot sooner, but I'd made that commitment to myself, and I wasn't about to let anything get in the way.

Classes at UCLA were a far cry from those at West Springfield High School. Most of my college classes were held in huge auditoriums, with a professor instructing from a stage, his voice echoing throughout the hall with the aid of a microphone.

Nancy Hogshead, the great swimmer who captured three gold medals at the 1984 Olympics, has described the Olympic Village as a "study in contrasts." She explains the picture of extremes among the athletes, from the smallest gymnast to the sturdiest weight lifter; from the leanest runner to the ruggedest wrestler. The UCLA campus was no different.

In one of my classes I sat beside Mark Eaton, a UCLA basketball star who later went on to become center for the Utah Jazz. Mark is so tall—well over seven feet—that when he sat in the auditorium he had to drape his legs over the row of seats in front of us. Me, on the other hand, well . . . my feet barely touched the floor in front of me. I noticed this contrast the first time we sat down. Mark and I shared a good laugh over it.

Even though I was on crutches I still managed to train somewhat. I needed to keep going; I needed to keep my dream in focus. But in addition to training, I tried to concentrate on something else which was important to me: my education.

As usual, I overdid it. That entire first semester it seems I was in a constant state of anxiety, overstudying, trying to remember every word each professor said, knowing, *knowing* I just had to learn everything in order to get decent grades. With my gymnastics career hanging by the thread of an ankle bone, I knew I'd better get the best grades possible.

By the time final exams arrived, I was terrified of failing.

One course that I took was Jazz. Peter and Donna were in the same class. We decided to study for the final together, along with a couple of girls who also were classmates. We ordered a pizza and sat around the floor, quizzing each other. But I had already studied (incessantly), and I was prepared.

"What was Dizzy Gillespie's wife's mother's maiden name?" I asked.

Silence fell over the room. Aha! They didn't know!

Peter finally broke the silence. "What?" he asked, straight-faced.

"Dizzy Gillespie. His wife's mother's maiden name."

"This is a joke, right?" one of the girls asked.

Then they all started to laugh. I guess they knew I was serious by the expression on my face.

"He mentioned it one day in class," I feebly tried to defend myself.

"Tim!" Peter couldn't stop laughing. "What did you do? Memorize every word the guy said for the last two and a half months?"

"Well," I said, now starting to think about how stupid I'd sounded. "Yes. God, I've never been to college before! How am I supposed to know what to expect?" I laughed along with them, but I was convinced they would all fail. Hadn't I been taught as a kid that you always had to go one step beyond others? That you had to build a better skating rink, or carry a four-hundred-dollar violin to make your costume the most authentic? I realized that I was applying those same principles of overachievement to my studying. But, deep down, I knew that Peter and the girls simply hadn't studied hard enough.

Well, the exam came and went, and the professor never asked Dizzy Gillespie's wife's mother's maiden name, or a lot of other things I knew cold. But I managed to do well anyway (as did Peter and the girls), and though I ended the semester with nearly a 4.0, I learned I really needed to stop stressing myself out quite so much on studying.

I finally got off crutches just before I went home for Christmas. It was so good to be home, back in my familiar environment, surrounded by noisy kids and constant commotion. Sheila, the "baby," was now eleven; twins Daniel and David were fourteen; Sharon was seventeen; Susan, nineteen; and Michael, twenty. Plus, Susan's boyfriend, Scott Parent, was now a "fixture" in the house, and it was like having another brother around.

Then, too, of course, there was Big Mac. Susan had taught him to answer the telephone. Whenever it rang, there were squeals and shouts through the house.

"Mac! Phone!"

Big Mac ran to the phone, reached up with one paw, knocked the receiver off the hook and to the floor. When it landed, he leaned over and let out a husky "Woof!" into the receiver.

Man, this place was getting wilder by the day!

The poly pillow business was booming, and though what had once been called the "big house" now seemed small with the overabundance of teenagers, things were actually running pretty well true to form. Except that it was getting harder to find a pair of socks that matched. In my absence my younger brothers had devised a method for diving into the clean laundry first and making off with all the socks they could find.

As much as I loved being home, after only one day I became a real twitch. I needed to work out. I spent the rest of my vacation driving between the gyms at Southern Connecticut State University and the University of Massachusetts in Amherst.

One night before I returned to L.A., everyone had gone to bed and I couldn't get to sleep. I was eager to get back to school. I went upstairs into the hall and did some stretching exercises against the wall, then went into a handstand. I was holding it there, braced against the wall in the dark hallway, thinking about getting back into full workouts now that I was off crutches. Just then my mother screamed. It startled me, and I fell to the floor. I looked up and she was staring at me. Even in the dark I could see she was furious.

"Timothy!" she screeched as she realized it was me. "You scared the life out of me!"

Uh oh. I was in trouble again. "Hi, Mom," I said quietly.

"What are you doing?" she whispered angrily.

"Just, you know. Thinking. Stretching."

"Will you please get back to bed like a normal person before you wake up everyone in the whole house?"

"Everyone *is* awake," one of my brothers said from behind a closed door.

"Well, now we know Timmy's home," one of my sisters echoed.

After the holidays it was back to school and back into training, *real* training, and it wasn't easy. I'd been pampering my ankle for so long, getting back was going to be a major undertaking.

One afternoon I was having a particularly exasperating routine on the pommel horse. I landed roughly, backed up against the wall and threw my arms over my head.

"*Arrgh!*" I cried out in frustration, smashing the wall behind me with my hands. Suddenly there was an incredible hollow, thunking sound behind me and a hunk of plaster crashed from the wall, leaving a huge, gaping hole. I guess my upper arm strength really *had* increased from my mini-workouts on the crutches. I stood there, feeling ridiculous, covered with crumbled plaster. The other guys stopped what they were doing to see what all the noise was about.

"Hey, Bull!" Peter shouted. "Try not to attack the walls like you attack the horse."

"Yeah, well, you guys can laugh, but I've finally made my mark in this gym!"

"Yeah, well, try to take it a little easier next month, okay?" Mitch laughed.

By "next month" Mitch was referring to the NCAA (National Collegiate Athletic Association) Championships, the first major meet I would be competing in since my ankle had been operated on, and the first major meet of my collegiate career.

After several weeks of training, I felt great again. My ankle had healed nicely (though I would still need to wear a brace for several months), and I'd regained all my strength, even adding to it a little more. But I wasn't surprised; I had never expected anything less. As for those who thought I didn't have what it takes, well, let's just say they were going to change their minds.

The meet finally arrived, and I was ready. I was doing fairly well in the competition, then came the floor exercise. The routine started.

First pass. I ran down the mat and flew through the air twice—in perfect pike position, landing squarely on my feet.

Second pass. I flawlessly flipped once and twisted twice, pressing to a rock solid handstand.

Third pass. The balance skill—the chance to steady my breathing, to eye the next target. I raised one leg, creating an exact "Y" scale.

This was going great. I had so much strength, and my timing was exact. Now for the dismount.

I raced across the mat once again and heaved myself forward, this time into a round-off, flip-flop, double-back. But somehow I got a little bit crooked in the air, and came down a little bit off. I landed and felt the pain. I looked down. I was staring at the bottom of my foot. My "good" ankle had rolled out and was completely dislocated.

Naturally the naysayers were back in full force. There was no way this kid—or his ankles—could ever make it.

This time, however, the doctors didn't think surgery was necessary, but they still put my ankle in a cast. The following week, the UCLA Men's Gymnastics Team was scheduled to go to Japan for a meet with several Japanese universities. I went, too—as did my cast, my crutches and my sometimes-too-positive attitude.

At the meet I competed on the pommel horse and the parallel bars, even doing a double-back off parallel bars and landing on my feet, cast and all. But what I was really eager to do was my routine on the high bar. Just before my left ankle went out I'd been practicing that new release skill called a "Gienger" (named after the German gymnast who first performed it in international competition, Eberhard Gienger). The Gienger is great—you let go of the bar, do a back flip, half-twist, then catch the bar again. I couldn't wait to show off my newly learned skill to the Japanese.

"No, Timmy, absolutely not," Mako said.

"Mr. Mako!" I protested.

"It's too dangerous for your ankle. And that's final."

I was so enthusiastic about competing that I resented Mako's decision. But watching the others go through their high bar routines, I knew he was right. The pressure of landing a dismount off the bar could have done permanent damage to my ankle. However, because I couldn't do all my routines, it meant the UCLA team was one competitor short. We lost the meet.

In May came the USA Championships. Though the cast had come off, I was now wearing a brace on my left ankle—it matched the brace I still needed on my right ankle—and I looked like anything but championship athlete material. But I had to compete at the Championships because they counted as the first qualifying meet for the World Championships to be held in October 1981.

I vaguely remember competing in the USA Championships; I don't even remember how I did. I do know that before each floor, vault and high bar routine, I layered tape over each ankle, put on the braces, then put more tape over the braces. On top of that went my shoes, then more tape. It was imperative to give my ankles as much stability as possible. I probably shouldn't have competed at all.

By the end of my freshman year I had become adept at studying entire college courses traveling from Los Angeles to New York and halfway around the world. It wasn't easy, but it worked. Unlike the myths surrounding some college athletes, gymnasts were not allowed to be pure "jocks." There was little glamour in being a gymnast, and if you wanted to compete at the college level, you had to maintain a solid grade point average.

With the end of freshman year also came the gymnastics banquet. It was that evening that Peter got behind the podium to "say a few words." Those few words included presenting me with a plaque—a shiny, polished mahogany award onto which had been affixed a piece of plaster from the wall in the gym. Beneath the plaster is an inscription:

To Tim "The Bull" Daggett—
with determination to make the walls come tumbling down.

We trained throughout the summer, sometimes in L.A., sometimes at USGF-affiliated camps in various parts of the country. I was eagerly awaiting September and the final trials for the World Championships. Another positive thing about September was that although I had to remain in the dorm, I was going to be rooming with Peter. At last! Someone who understood my psyche! Someone who knew the difference between sleep time and party time! Someone who carried into the room the aroma of chalk dust instead of beer!

Throughout the summer we trained like crazy, hell-bent on putting in a great showing at the final trials.

By the time September rolled around, I still needed to tape both ankles. For the pommel horse, rings and parallel bars I needed only one layer of tape; for the other events I still needed layer upon layer. My feet looked like those of an ailing racehorse. But I was determined to compete, and determined to make the team.

For the World Championship team there are eight qualifiers—six on the competing team and two alternates. I fought to make it all the way. In event after event, I did the very best I could, landing as perfectly as possible on my braced ankles, never giving in to the pain, looking as solid and steady as a rock. Then, after each event, like many injured athletes, I limped away from the apparatus.

Incredibly, I finished sixth and made the team. What was even more surprising to me was that Mitch Gaylord, who was so much more talented, only finished eighth, and ended up a team alternate. That's when I realized how important it is sometimes to be a little bit dumb to adversity. I probably should have thought that because Mitch was so much better than I was that I didn't have a chance to make the team. After all, I was struggling with an injury. But by focusing on myself alone, I came out a victor.

This is one area in which gymnastics differs from other, more popular sports. When we train and compete as a team, as I did with Mitch for UCLA, the glory of the team dominates. But each of us remains an individual competitor, too. The only way in gymnastics (as in diving) to beat your competitor is by perfecting your individual performance, not by throwing a faster punch or pulling down a rebound. Because Mitch was my teammate and my friend I felt badly that he hadn't made the competitive team—but I learned that when you're winning it's because someone else is losing. I hated it when it was one of my friends who was losing.

We traveled to Moscow for the 1981 World Championships in October. Man, was I psyched! I was nineteen years old, and it looked as though my dream was starting to fall into place. That year the World Championships, then a year off from international competition, then another World Championships in 1983, and then . . . then, the dream—the 1984 Olympic Games. I was so psyched up. I was so ready. For the first time, I was good enough to compete with the greatest athletes in the world.

I clutched my passport as though my very life depended on it (some lessons I learned well!), and because of my pumping adrenaline I hardly noticed the grayness of the city or the cold chill in the air. We went to our hotel, then were bused to the Soviet Sports Complex. The huge arena, which had been the setting for the 1980 Olympics, was overwhelming. We walked in to the arena for warm-ups, and Peter stopped. He looked around.

"This is where it didn't happen," he said to me quietly. There was a little sadness in his voice, the somberness of disappointment. But in an instant I could see his attitude change. He gave a small sigh, an "everything is going to be fine" smile, and we headed off to warm-ups.

Before the meet I was having a hard time controlling my excitement. Between meeting so many new people, seeing so many familiar faces and giving my brace to Li Ning, the emotion of the meet was tremendously fulfilling. Just being there was exhilarating.

During the competition I was really doing well for the United States. The last event of the meet was the vault—the one event which, I'll admit, has never been my favorite. It seems like all the training gets squeezed into too short a time span. In only a few seconds you run down the runway, hit the board, use one skill, then, bam, it's over.

Well, whether it was my dislike for the event or the huge rush of adrenaline that I couldn't seem to keep under control, I'll never know . . . but something, somehow, pushed me to do what would become the most embarrassing routine of my career.

I was first up for the USA. I would be doing the compulsory Yamashita vault with a half-twist—it's like a handspring, where you dive over the horse and flip once, touching the horse, then you push off and pike. It becomes a handspring, pike, open, half-turn and land. A simple vault. But because everyone does the same vault, I knew I had to do it great, with tremendous height and precision power.

With my energy surging, I ran down the runway. As soon as I hit the board I knew I had been running too fast, I had far too much power. I couldn't handle it. I flew into the air completely out of control. I knew if I piked I'd rotate even faster and start flipping, ultimately landing in a toppled mess on the mat.

I had to make an instantaneous judgment: I decided not to pike. I tumbled down to the mat, still completely out of control, and landed on the edge of the podium, looking squarely into the bewildered faces of the judges.

Mako was on the floor and he turned to Abie Grossfeld.

"That was warm-ups, right?"

Abie grimaced. "Nope. That was it."

They both groaned, but couldn't help laughing. I know I must have looked hysterical flying through the air out of control! I ran off the podium and quickly sat down. I couldn't believe I had done that. In fact, it was so funny, neither could anyone else. I'm surprised the guys didn't change my name from "The Bull" to "Rocket Man."

There was some discrepancy in my score: the Russian judge wanted to give me a "0". After a brief conference the judges ended up giving me a 7.75—which is just as bad!

We finished the competition with the USA in fifth place—a great showing against all our competitors. But now I knew exactly how much work we had cut out for us. We still had three years before the Olympics, and we were going to beat them all. I just knew it.

Beyond all the excitement over world-class competition, academics still loomed as another priority. In my sophomore year, following the suggestion of my teammates, I went to speak to each professor immediately following the first class. I explained that because I had made the World team I would be traveling quite a lot, and I wanted to set up a schedule for my work so I wouldn't fall behind. They were all very cooperative about this, often preparing a detailed syllabus of the course content for me, and letting me know well in advance what exams and papers would be expected of me. As I mentioned before, there were no "favors" for gymnasts; it was up to us to find the ways to complete our courses.

The second semester of my sophomore year there was, however, one instructor who didn't want to hear it.

I knew the USA/China meet would be coming in the spring of 1982, and I needed to have my studies worked out so I could realistically schedule training. What made matters even worse, on the first day of class I discovered that the final exam for that course was going to be held from 3:00 to 6:00 P.M.—on the same day as the meet.

Though the competition was to be at 7:00 P.M. and in Los Angeles, I knew there was no way I could take the exam the same day.

"When you sign up for a class you sign a contract," the instructor said. He took out his daily planner and added, "I suggest you get yourself one of these. You are here to study."

According to him there was "no situation where one can miss a final exam" of his.

I lost my cool.

"Does that mean if my father died I'd still have to take it from 3:00 to 6:00 P.M.?"

"Precisely," he answered. "Just because you're an athlete doesn't give you the right to expect favors."

There was that word again.

"Believe me," I said, "favors are the last thing I expect. I know better."

The night before the competition, there was a huge party in the dorm. Many students were finished with their finals, and to them "school was out." I was trying to study, and I knew I had to get some sleep before the meet. It was that night that Peter and I decided we would find a way to live in an apartment the following year.

I took my final exam, rushed to Pauley Pavilion and warmed up. Surprisingly, I did pretty well in the meet, and even got a B in the class.

Then Peter and I went apartment hunting, and luckily found one near the gym. It was small and cramped, but over the next few years it became an international apartment of sorts, as we played host to many gymnasts from other countries who came to train at UCLA— including the Danish national champion, Henrik Berdelson and "Kit" Kitagowa, one of Japan's top gymnasts.

From that summer of 1982 until the summer of 1983, the time flew. The days were never long enough; there never seemed to be enough time to study or train. In May of 1983 Peter graduated from school, and shortly after that he and Donna were married. He was the first of us to make the "really big" commitment, and I was honored that he asked me to be his Best Man.

For the past couple of years, it seemed that Donna had made it a priority to fix me up with every roommate and friend she could find. But now, as the Olympics loomed even closer, my sole focus on gymnastics made it nearly impossible for me to unwind and have a good time. I envied Peter and Donna their ability to develop a solid relationship together through the training, and before the total craziness that was to follow.

Mako—always the good sport!—gave Peter three days off for his honeymoon. Then it was back into training, first for the 1983 World Championships, which were held that fall. Next we focused on the year ahead of us: preparation, at last, for the Olympic Games.

7

And so it began: day after day, practicing each routine exactly as I would perform it in the Olympics; night after night, going over each routine in my head, sticking my dismounts again and again. The weeks, the months, flew by. I became totally focused on my dream, kept my class schedule to a minimum and rarely socialized: this was to be the year of the ultimate sacrifice, for this was the year my dream would come true.

We were practicing in a new gym now—the John Wooden Center at UCLA. The gym was bright and sunny, but we hardly noticed. It was only the apparatus that mattered, only our concentration. Each day we knew what we had to accomplish; each night Peter and I knew we had to take that extra step.

"It's the last event of the team competition," Peter announced. "Tim Daggett is up next. And he needs a perfect 10 for the team to beat the Chinese."

I went through my routine, then we reversed roles.

"It's the last event of the team competition," I announced. "Peter Vidmar is up next . . ."

The repetition kept us focused. The repetition that later would solidify our dreams.

I began to know each piece of apparatus as though it were part of my own body. I became one with the soft, supple touch of the leathery pommel horse, the rigid firmness of the rings, the speed of each rush of air as I spun giant swings around the high bar. I welcomed the solitude of the floor routine—the one event that uses no apparatus and demands only an unbreakable bond between you and the floor mats. I learned to pace each step of my vault, to train my legs to take so many steps, so far apart, always, always at the same speed. I studied the preparation for the parallel bars, coating them with a sugar-water combination, dusting them with chalk, determining the exact amount of time I needed to prepare the bars to achieve the perfect consistency to assure my grip. In all the years I had been doing gymnastics, I had never come close to this kind of sensitivity for and connection with the apparatus. I learned every rhythm for each touch; I grew to sense each vibration and to know each flexibility with which every piece of equipment would respond when I performed the skills.

Then, at last, it was May 1984. Time to fly to Chicago to compete in the USA Championships—the first trials, which count as 30 percent of the total score needed to make the Olympic team. Man, was I scared.

"Piece of cake," Peter tried to reassure me.

"No problem," Mitch agreed.

It was easy for them to say. They knew they'd have no trouble making the team. Although for the past four years I too had been in the top group of U.S. gymnasts, I knew I was only one slip, one miss, one stumble on a dismount away from not making the team. Even with all the confidence I'd gained over the years there was still a small part of me that would creep to the surface every so often and whisper:

This just can't happen to me. This is just not possible. I'm only a small-town boy from West Springfield, Massachusetts.

Now that we were in Chicago I tried to push those thoughts away, knowing they served no useful purpose, sensing that they would only undermine my performance.

Our first night there we went out for dinner as a group, and somehow ended up in a run-down part of the city. I was aware there were "street people" in the world, though I'd never been confronted by one.

I knew when the first one approached, he was going to ask me for a quarter—isn't that what they did? I reached into my jeans and fumbled for my change.

"Hey buddy, got a dollar?" the poor soul asked.

I was stunned.

"A *dollar?*" I asked.

"Yeah, man. A buck."

I quickly pulled my hand out of my pocket. "Sorry, pal." I guess I was naive to inflation, but to me, a dollar was too hard to come by.

That night, thankfully, I slept well. One of my greatest nightmares was that sleep would elude me just before an important meet, and I'd be too tired to perform well. But in the morning, relaxed and feeling good, I knew I would have no excuse for not doing my best.

The competition was scheduled as in other big meets: first day, compulsories; then a day off; then the optionals. At the end of the optionals, the top eighteen gymnasts would qualify to go on to the final trials in June.

The arena was at Northwestern University. We drove there from our hotel and started warming up. By the time the compulsory competition began I felt pretty good—still nervous, but more confident.

But in gymnastics, as in life, sometimes you just never know. Things have a way of happening—or not happening—when you least expect them. I did terribly in the compulsories, finishing only tenth. If I maintained that position after the optionals it would still be good enough to go on to the final trials, but it was not good enough for me. It was sort of like being ahead at halftime in the Super Bowl. It really wasn't worth a damn.

"It's a long meet, Timmy," Mako rationalized. "It's only half over. Don't get caught up in the thought that you're losing, or you will."

He was right. Before I went to sleep I remembered my first attempt at the Junior Nationals in Colorado. I thought about how I was determined to let that enormous defeat work to my advantage; certainly I could do it again. Sure, this time the stakes were higher, but I hadn't been defeated yet, and I wasn't going to be.

On our "day off" we worked out physically. I worked, too, at readjusting my attitude. "This is it. This is the first step to your dream. Dreams can come true, even to you," I told myself over and over.

That night Mako decided to take us to a movie. Unlike some of the other coaches, Mako always worked at keeping us focused. He didn't take us to just any movie simply to pass the time, he took us to see *The Natural*, starring Robert Redford.

The movie was a great inspiration. It is the story of an incredibly talented baseball player trying to make it to the top. I remember one part in particular when a young Roy Hobbs (Redford's character) was practicing with his father.

"You've got a gift, Roy," his father said. "But it's not enough. You've got to develop yourself. Rely too much on your gift and you'll fail."

When we went back to the hotel, I knew that the next day would be different. I was not going to take my experience for granted; I was going to work my damnedest to put in a perfect showing.

The first event in the optionals was the rings. I knew if I didn't do well, I might have a hard time qualifying. I planned to do a triple flyaway for my dismount—a difficult dismount, which no one else was doing. But I had to do it; I had to do it for me. It worked. I nailed the dismount and got a 9.85.

I looked over and saw Bart Conner from Oklahoma doing the floor exercise. Bart was a terrific gymnast and was way ahead of me in the standings. But he was trying to come back from a recent injury—a torn bicep—and at the end of his routine he wobbled, toppling face-first into the floor. I felt a tremendous pull in my gut. I could not imagine his frustration. Bart was now twenty-six and, having missed out on the 1980 Olympics, this was his last chance at the gold. But his body was betraying him, and he ended up having to pull out of the competition.

Witnessing how quickly a gymnast's life can change, I gave it all I had. My optional routines got stronger and stronger, and in the last event—the pommel horse—I scored a perfect 10, putting me in fourth place overall, behind Mitch, Peter and Nebraska's Jim Hartung. I was halfway to the Olympic Games.

For the next month it was all business. Although I had finished fourth at the Championships, that still only counted as 30 percent toward making the team. I had to be strong for the final trials; I had to be the best that I could be.

The trials were held in Jacksonville, Florida, and they were going to be televised. It was rare then for gymnastics to be shown to millions of people—it made me a little nervous, but then, it would be good preparation for the Olympics. *If* I made it.

When we got to Jacksonville, Mako rented a station wagon to cart us around. We were being housed in gorgeous condominiums, but we were far from any restaurants. God knows, none of us was about to cook.

The night before the competition, we piled into the car to go get some dinner. I was getting into the back when Mako, his mind certainly on the competition, stepped on the gas. I fell out of the car and smacked my head on the pavement.

"Stop!" one of the guys screamed.

Mako slammed on the brakes.

"Tim fell out!"

The chaos that ensued was like something out of a *Three Stooges* episode, with everyone scrambling to the back of the car to see what had happened and Mako flying from the driver's seat and running frantically to the back. I was fine ("hard-headed" anyway, the guys agreed), but Mako was devastated. Actually, though, the little "accident" helped to cut some of the tension we were all feeling.

"Olympic hopeful found dead at the hands of his coach," one of the guys said.

"Tim Daggett couldn't make the trials because he didn't have the head for it!" another one commented.

We ended up laughing all the way to dinner.

The next morning we did our usual morning training—running, stretching, conditioning—trying to act as if it was an ordinary day. We went out for breakfast and I ordered an English muffin, and, as always, took a jar of peanut butter from my bag. Did you ever notice that most restaurants don't have peanut butter? Though I was never one for a big breakfast I wanted my peanut butter! The only way to get it, I learned, was to bring it.

I was also never one for concentrating on nutrition. Unlike many athletes who make a regimented diet an important part of their training, I never did. Hey, I like cheeseburgers as much as the next guy, and I think pizza is one of the greatest foods invented. (We won't even *talk* about French fries!) I was, however, careful about what I ate during training, but wasn't religious about it. Some people have commented to me that maybe if I'd been more in tune with nutrition I would have done even better; I think I didn't need one more thing to think about! Training was my one and only focus, and in that sense I was totally "one-dimensional." If I'd been too cautious about my diet— planning, preparing and measuring all the "'right" foods—I think it would have taken away from my focus. Physically it might have given me an extra edge, but mentally it might have taken something away.

After breakfast we went to the arena for a workout. All eighteen qualifiers were there, plus Bart, who had successfully petitioned the USGF to void his appearance at the USA Championships because of his injury, and count 100 percent of his score at these final trials toward making the team. After workout we went back to the condos and I did what I did before every important meet—took a nap.

Two hours before the compulsories were to start, we returned to the arena for warm-ups. We walked in and the first thing I noticed was the people: my god, the stands were almost filled! Did this mean that the American public was becoming enthusiastic about gymnastics? Wow. It was overwhelming.

My father was there; Coach Jones was there: my brothers, Michael, Daniel, David, and sister Sheila were there. There wouldn't be enough money for all the kids to go to the Olympics: this trip was "theirs" as compensation for that. Knowing they were there lifted my spirits. My family's support had grown so important to me.

The competition was awesome. I breezed through the compulsories with an average score of 9.75; two days later during the optionals I finished with better than a 9.8 average. I remember the last routine of the optionals, the high bar. As I flew through the air and stuck my dismount, an overpowering feeling of accomplishment shot through me. I raised my arms to the judges and trembled all over with excitement. I had done it. I not only had done it, but I had finished second in the final trials, a hairbreadth behind Peter. Mitch came in third, but when our scores were combined with the 30 percent from the Championships, Mitch bumped me out of second and I ended up third. Jim Hartung was fourth, with Bart and Scott Johnson completing the team; Jim Mikus was named alternate.

Scoring, percentages, first, second or third . . . wow . . . Peter, Mitch, me—first, second and third! All of us from UCLA. Was this the same school I had doubts about so long ago? But it wasn't until we were going back to our room that night that the details were finally swept away and the reality hit me: my god, *I* had made the Olympic team. The kid from the small town had really done it.

Because the Games were to be held in Los Angeles, we returned there to train as a team. I didn't go back to my apartment, however: in order to keep our concentration totally on the Olympics, we were housed in a hotel. I roomed with Bart.

We had one month to train, which, needless to say, was the most exciting time of my life. Not only was my dream coming into focus, but I also had something completely new to me: money. Beyond our housing costs, we were given a thirty-five-dollar per diem by the USGF. I was rich! But the same part of me that had existed on twenty dollars that first summer in L.A. came back to haunt me, and I didn't want to spend a dime. Bart, however, felt differently.

Four years older, Bart was already financially secure: he had been doing exhibitions, TV commentary and other public appearances, and though a portion of the money he earned went to the USGF to retain his amateur status—well, let's put it this way, he drove a *Porsche!*

Every morning the hotel featured a lavish breakfast buffet for $12.95, and every morning Bart ordered it. Being the youngest team member and, of course, being a little in awe of Bart's success, I did what probably most anyone would do. I ordered the buffet, too. My thirty-five dollars quickly dwindled to twenty-two dollars, and the worst part was that I didn't even eat very much. But for the first time in my life, I felt like a star.

All the time we were training I was unaware of what was happening back in West Springfield. For one thing, my sister Sharon had been fired from her summer job for the town's park and recreation department. Though she had worked there every summer for four years, this year at the orientation meeting she mentioned she would need to take the week of the Olympics off. She said her brother was competing and she was going to go to Los Angeles. The following day she got a phone call.

"If you need to take that week off, we can't have you working for us this year."

Sharon was crushed. Not only did she love the job working with kids, but she needed the money for college. She immediately set out to apply for a waitressing position and began combing all the restaurants in town.

The next day she arrived home after yet another interview. There was a message for her.

"Call Kathy Tobin at Channel 40," the note read.

"Me?" she said out loud. "Why does Channel 40 want to talk to me?"

After some hesitation and considerable doubt, Sharon placed the call.

"We understand you've been fired from your job and won't be able to go to the Olympics to watch your brother compete," the reporter said.

Sharon was dumbfounded. She related the story, and the next day the publicity started with a fury. Front page of the newspaper; television and radio stations; the story was even picked up by the *New York Times* and the *Los Angeles Times*. The local police union and several anonymous town businessmen spearheaded a fund-raising drive; a Springfield radio station broadcasted "updates" of the situation daily and secured round-trip tickets from American Airlines. She was also hired as a summer employee by the Hampden County Register of Probate, with one week's unpaid vacation. By the time the Olympics arrived, the unheralded generosity of so many of our "neighbors" resulted in enough money for all the kids to go to the Games.

I, however, was not aware that my sister was actually receiving more press than I was! My family didn't want to bother me with the "details"—they felt there was enough time for that after the competition. They wanted me to focus only on what I had to do.

It was also not until after the Olympics that my mom told me she and my dad were divorced. Problems with the business, problems at home, had led to the breakup; it had been in the works for many months. They hadn't wanted to tell me, hadn't wanted to do anything to upset me during this most important year of my career. God, the support of my family simply never stopped, not even through the most difficult times.

As the Games drew closer, the entire city became transformed. There was constant activity everywhere, from the hotel lobby to the most isolated side street, as people from all over the world descended upon the City of Angels. Our training time was over: we had done all that we could, now it was time to show our stuff.

On July 14, 1984, we moved into the Olympic Village.

That's me in the middle — the shortest kid on the team. So much for dreams of the NBA.

My memento of "determination to make the walls come tumbling down."

1983–84 UCLA Men's Gymnastics Team. *Front row, left to right:* Head Coach Art Shurlock, Tom Rouse, Kirby Real, Tim Daggett, Mark Miyoaka, Chris Caso and Assistant Coach Makoto Sakamoto; *second row, left to right:* Jeff Dodson, Robbie Campbell, Alex Schwartz, Peter Vidmar and Luc Teurlings; *third row, left to right:* Mitch Gaylord, Mark Caso, Rich Tower and Eric Gaspard. *(Terry O'Donnell/ ASUCLA Photography)*

Competing for UCLA on the pommel horse — my favorite event. *(Norm Schindler/ASUCLA Photography)*

Pre-Olympic pensiveness! *(Springfield Union-News/Photo by Michael Gordon)*

A gymnast's dream: scoring a perfect "10" at the Olympic Games. Head Coach Abie Grossfeld shares my excitement. *(Scott Thode/U.S. News & World Report)*

The gold was ours! *Left to right:* Bart Conner, Peter Vidmar, Jim Hartung, Mitch Gaylord, Scott Johnson and me. *(Ken Regan/ABC Sports Camera 5)*

My proud grandparents, Charles and Florence Shields, raise the American flag at home after we won the gold. *(Springfield Union-News/ Photo by Mark M. Murray)*

The homecoming parade in West Springfield, Massachusetts. *(Springfield Union-News/Photo by Dave Roback)*

Me with the greatest dog a guy could ever have, Big Mac. *(© Boston Herald/Arthur Pollock)*

Moments after my leg shattered at the 1987 World Championships in Rotterdam, Holland. *(AP/Wide World Photos)*

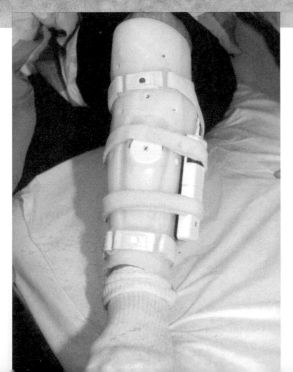

My state-of-the-art cast/bone stimulator that allowed me to go back into training within weeks of the injury. *(Dr. Bert Mandelbaum)*

Me with my coach, Yefim Furman—who was always there when I needed him. *(Reprinted with permission, IG Photos)*

The scar says it all. *(James A. Langone)*

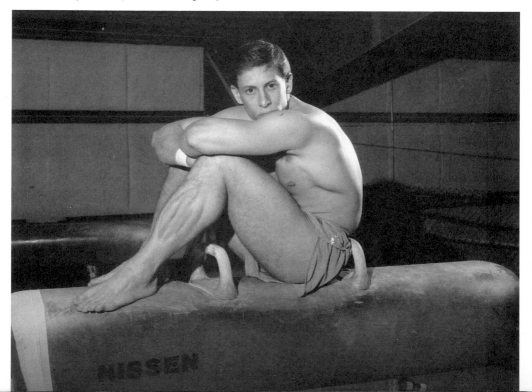

Training for the 1988 Olympic Trials. *(Neil Leifer/Time Magazine)*

Coming full circle, together again: me with Coach Bill Jones — the man who started it all — in the training pit at Tim Daggett Gold Medal Gymnastics. *(Marc Rohrbacher)*

Me with my mom, Connie Daggett.
(James A. Langone)

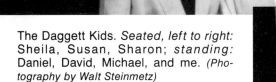

The Daggett Kids. *Seated, left to right:* Sheila, Susan, Sharon; *standing:* Daniel, David, Michael, and me. *(Photography by Walt Steinmetz)*

My nephew, Ryan Scott Parent, loves to see his Uncle Tim stand on his hands.

8

Being in the Village was indescribable. Athletes from all over the world began arriving, and the energy force of these thousands of highly motivated individuals charged the air.

The U.S. Men's Gymnastics Team was housed in an apartment that overlooked the competition pool for the swimmers. Each day we awoke to the sound of bodies slicing into the water, breaking the morning stillness. It was exhilarating.

The opening ceremonies were to be held the night before our first competition. We knew we might be tired if we went to the ceremonies, and we actually debated about not going. But, man, we really wanted to. We finally decided that, as a team, we had to go. It was an experience we shouldn't miss, tired or not.

We walked over as a group from the sports arena, through a dark tunnel. Suddenly a burst of sunlight came through the entrance—sunlight splashed with a kaleidoscope of colors—bright, vivid colors of the flags and banners of nations around the globe, rippling through the breeze, heralded by the cheers of the crowd. Then I heard it: the Olympic theme song. I heard every note, every emotional refrain.

Suddenly it was no longer just a sound stuck in the head of a little boy; it was for real this time, and they were playing it for me.

At that instant, my dream came true.

I walked into the stadium and there they were: ninety thousand screaming people. Mako was beside me. I thought about things he had said throughout this past year of training: "It's going to be tough. It's going to be hell to make it."

As though he could read my mind, Mako turned to me and smiled.

"Well, Timmy, you made it."

My eyes filled with tears.

Late that night we crawled into bed exhausted from the excitement yet anxious about the next day's competition. During the night, my emotions caught up with me. Sound asleep, I jumped from my bunk and crossed the floor to Bart, who had the unfortunate luck to have the bed next to mine.

"Bart! Bart!" I screamed into his face. "Wake up! We've got to move the heavy stuff in here!" That said, I went calmly back to my bunk and continued sleeping.

Of course, once again I remembered nothing about this in the morning. But Bart did. When he told the others they laughed. They had all been victims of my late-night outbursts at one time or another.

Somehow we managed to get through the next day, and when we walked into Pauley Pavilion for warm-ups that evening, I was struck by the changeover of the arena. What had always looked to me like just another arena now was gorgeous: there were flowers of every color of the rainbow, carpeting around the podium, banners and flags every-where. And there were people. More people than I'd ever seen at any meet anywhere in the world.

There are four nights of Men's Gymnastics competition in the Olympic Games, with a "day off" in between. The first night, Sunday, July 29, was the Team Compulsories; next, Tuesday, July 31, was the Team Optionals. Scores from those two nights were added together to determine the Team winners. The third night, Thursday, August 2, was the Individual All-Around, in which the top thirty-six scorers of the first two nights—with a maximum of three gymnasts from any given country—competed for the gold, silver and bronze based on the combined scores of the three nights. The fourth night, Saturday, August 4, was the Men's Individual Finals, in which the top eight scorers on the individual apparatus during the first two nights of competition—with a maximum of two gymnasts from any given country—competed for individual apparatus medals.

That night, the Team Compulsories began, and the world was watching. We were starting on rings. I was exhausted; I felt like a slug.

Whether from the supercharge of adrenaline, the immense pressure, or a combination of both (I later learned that many athletes go through the same thing), when the time comes to compete, you feel like you can't get out of your own way. My body was limp. I wasn't sure I could walk over to the apparatus, never mind perform a move even as simple as an iron cross.

My name was called. I walked up on the platform and saluted the judge.

"Well, here we go," I thought, taking the deepest breath I could manage. "This is what you've waited thirteen years for. Now, for God's sake, Daggett, try and stay awake."

I was lifted up to the rings, and suddenly, with that first contact with the familiar fiberglass, the energy kicked in. I exploded through my routine, feeling stronger and more capable than ever.

The Chinese had already competed on the rings, but none of us had been paying attention to their scores; we were too intent on starting. I did pretty well on the event, as did all the guys on our team.

Then Jim Mikus came running over to us.

"You're not going to believe this, but you're three-tenths ahead of the Chinese!" he said.

We stood there and looked at him. Wordlessly, we looked at each other. Holy cow. The Chinese were historically very strong on rings. Maybe we could do something here after all.

The next event was vaulting, my least favorite compulsory. I did okay, though, scoring a 9.75. Then it was on to the parallel bars, where I had a decent routine and scored a 9.8.

Mitch was up after me. I watched him give a flawless performance. But he thought otherwise. Before his score was posted he came over and flopped down beside me.

"How was it, Tim? Man, it really felt bad."

"Bad? Are you kidding? It was great!" I tried to reassure him, but he shook his head. Because you're concentrating so hard on your routine, you often can't judge for yourself how you did. You can make a major flaw and not even know; you can do everything right and have no idea. Mitch really believed he'd had a bad routine. He scored a perfect 10.

We all finished with healthy scores, and Jim Mikus reported the latest statistic: after the first three events, we had increased our lead to seven-tenths over the Chinese. This was getting scary.

High bar was next, and I had my best score so far, a 9.9. Again, Mitch followed me. One of the objects of the compulsory high bar routine is to go right into a handstand after mounting the bar. You need to do it to get a high score, but if you try to do it really well, you can fall the wrong way. It's nerve-racking. In the four years Mitch and I had trained together at UCLA, I had never, *never* seen him fall the wrong way. I, however, had done it many times, as had most of the guys I trained with. But not Mitch. Not until that night.

When Mitch "went over" it stunned us. Reality set in. We might have a slight lead over the Chinese, but on any event, at any time, any one of us could make a major mistake like this.

I put myself in Mitch's place, knowing the last thing I'd want to hear was "It's okay, Mitch, it'll be fine." I knew it wouldn't be "fine," and, what's more, I knew Mitch knew it. When he came and sat down I just said, "Hey, what can you do? Let's just get it from here on out."

Floor exercise went well for all of us; then came the final event of the compulsories, the pommel horse. I knew we'd do well here, too— this had always been a strong event for every one of us. But I was worried, because recently, Scott had been having a real hard time with his first skill, the mount.

That's a problem in gymnastics. Like Scott, you can be really good at something for a long, long time. Then, seemingly for no reason, you start to have trouble with one stupid skill. After a while it becomes almost like a losing streak for a baseball team; the harder you try, the less success you have.

We sat nervously, waiting for Scott's routine. He saluted the judge and went to the horse. He did his mount—it was perfect! His confidence renewed, Scott went on to do a great routine. When he was finished, we all felt as though we had won.

This is one advantage we had in 1984, which I think is what led us to the gold: we really cared about each other, we were really a *team*. Unlike the teams from many other countries, we were not focused on individual performances. If someone was having a problem on a certain skill we all knew it, and we all tried to help. We suffered along with one another when there was a problem; we all felt the victory when each one of us succeeded. Although we basically were competitors with each other, first and foremost we were a team.

Energized by Scott's performance, Peter put in a spectacular pommel horse routine, and scored a 10; then I "flaired" my way easily through, too, getting a 9.95. We were charged. We ended the night ahead of the favorites—the Chinese and the Japanese.

I swear the next two days were the longest of my life. Waiting for the Team Optionals was unbearable. What made matters worse was that the press had come out of the woodwork, and the media was something we weren't accustomed to. After all, gymnastics had never been a top priority among sports enthusiasts.

But we were winning! Us—the underdogs, the hometown boys—we were actually winning. The pressure that that added on us was indescribable. We knew the team competition was only halfway finished; we knew we had a long way to go to really win. We *thought* we could do it, but the press was really pushing. They were comparing us to the 1980 USA Hockey Team; they were hyping each and every one of us to no end. And they were setting us, and the entire country, up for a major disappointment if we failed.

The optionals did not start off well. Because we were leading, we were able to do the exact Olympic order of events—floor, pommel horse, rings, vault, parallel bars and high bar. This should have been a benefit; it was the same rotation we had practiced for so many years.

I was first up on floor, an event that was never great for me since the beginning of my ankle problems. I was doing a very difficult skill—a double layout—something few other gymnasts were doing. It was risky. I'd only used it in competition a few times, and each time I'd made a mistake. It would have been easier not to do it—I could have assured myself the chance for a higher score by doing a different skill that I was more comfortable with, but I'd made another one of those weird commitments to myself just before the Games that *no matter what happened*, I would do my routines *exactly* as I'd practiced. I was not going to "water down" anything. This might be my only chance at the Olympics, and I had to do it for myself. It was a matter of pride.

I made the double layout. But I had been so worried about it that I messed up on another skill and ended up with a 9.5. Ugh. Not a great way to get the team started.

The other guys followed and did decently, but not terrifically. Almost everyone's scores were lower than usual. The pressure was beginning to show.

Next event was the pommel horse. Peter and I both got a 9.9, but the other guys were not as great as they usually were. Meanwhile, the Chinese were doing great, and were quickly closing the gap.

Then I was faced with another decision: should I, or shouldn't I, do the risky triple-back on the rings? If I didn't make it, I could really hurt the team. But, once again, it was the skill I'd been practicing for so long, and then there was my commitment to myself. I knew I had to do it. Besides, if I made it I'd get a higher score and that would help the team. I made it. And, as with Scott's "victory" on the pommel horse mount during the compulsories, I think it helped recharge the team. Scott, Peter, Jim and Bart all put in great routines . . . and Mitch scored a 10. We were getting hot again.

We blew through the vault and the parallel bars. Bart scored a 10 on the parallel bars, which was a big boost. He did the best routine I'd ever seen him do, including a beautiful double-back, and he stuck his dismount.

There was one event left: the high bar. It was our chance. Our last chance. Our only chance. We were less than two-tenths ahead of the Chinese. The crowd was going wild.

"U-S-A! U-S-A!" The chants had begun.

We went over to the high bar and I reached into my bag, taking out my wrist wraps—those same wraps I used when I won my first State title so long ago. I blocked out the sounds of the crowd, and carefully began winding the familiar cotton around my wrists, thinking about how far these seemingly inconsequential pieces of material had come with me: over the years they had become symbols of my commitment to my sport. I taped the wraps, then slipped the cut-off socks over them. Yes, there were more "technical" wristbands on the market, but I didn't want to use them. No manufactured product could possibly hold the meaning that mine had come to have for me. They had served me through many great routines; they would certainly serve me well through this last important event. It wasn't superstition; it was a matter of tradition.

Scott was up first. He was doing a very difficult routine, ending with a triple-back dismount. He was doing great, but he opened up a little early on his dismount, and put both hands down on the mat. We went into shock. He got a 9.5. With our small lead, this meant we would all have to be as perfect as possible, no slips, no flaws, no mistakes.

Jim was next. Talk about pressure! But the great Nebraska Corn-Husker came through with a super routine and got a 9.8.

Next came Bart. I remember thinking, "Man, come on. Just one more routine, Bart." He was great and got a 9.9.

Then it was Mitch. He planned to use his *Gaylord II*—a very risky release move that he had missed in the Olympic Trials. I'm sure he debated whether or not he should do it . . . but, like me, it was something he had prepared for, something he *had* to do. He flew away from the bar, and I almost wanted to close my eyes. But then, my god, he *caught* the bar. The crowd went out of control. He got a 9.95.

Then it was my turn. And the rest, as they say, is history.

PART II

BEYOND THE DREAM

9

was dizzy with excitement. After the awards ceremony they whisked us from the arena out toward the John Wooden Center for a press conference. There was a skywalk connecting Pauley Pavilion to the Center, and as we approached the exit, the sounds of the crowd swelled.

"*U-S-A! U-S-A!*"

We had left the arena behind. Why were the chants getting louder?

That's when we saw them. Beneath the skywalk and all over the grounds were thousands of people—people who hadn't even been in the arena, people who had found out about our victory, and were there to cheer us on. I had never experienced anything like it, and I remember thinking that this is what a "mob scene" is. And it was for us!

We made it to the press conference, walking in to a standing ovation. Somehow my mom talked the guards into letting her in; Peter's parents did, too. I saw them through the crowd of reporters and cameras—I don't know who was smiling more, us or them. They were all so proud.

Peter tried explaining to the press the irony of how he and I had trained, how each night we had visualized our final routines exactly as it had happened that night. Even I had to admit it sounded a little farfetched. Had we actually imagined it so perfectly? Could that possibly be true? We had, after all, been given little or no hope of even winning a team medal at the Games. I don't think they believed us.

After the press conference we were piled into vans and went by police escort to the ABC studios in L.A. to be interviewed by Frank Gifford and Kathleen Sullivan. It was wild! While waiting for the show to begin, I sat next to Frank Gifford. I have always admired Frank—in addition to seeming to be such a good guy, he always made it a point to do a wonderful job covering gymnastics. I couldn't believe I was sitting there making small talk with him. He was so excited for us. The studio had put together a series of clips from our performances, and when we went on the air, they cued it in.

"Okay, guys," Frank said. "This is for you."

The title of the piece was "We Are the Champions." As we sat in the studio watching, it crystallized the accomplishment for us. We really *had* won. This was the first of many experiences when the truth would hit home. Because, all these years later, sometimes I still have a hard time believing this really happened.

We were then quickly split up to make appearances at different studios: Bart and I were to go to NBC for a "Today Show" segment. We were driven in a limousine . . . complete with television, bar and a telephone. Even Bart didn't have a phone in his Porsche, so we started calling everyone we could think of.

My mom and the kids were staying in Santa Ana at the home of Dan Grissette and his wife, Judy. Judy is a West Springfield native and they generously gave them the house for their trip to L.A. I tried to call them. There was no answer. I tried to call Coach Jones at his hotel room. There was no answer. I tried calling everyone I knew in the L.A. area . . . no one was home! What a bummer. My first night of stardom and I couldn't get through to anyone.

After the taping we all met back at the 32nd Street Cafe (except for Peter, who had the good sense to go home), a small place across from the Olympic Village. It was packed with screaming, laughing, joyful people. The only sound that could be heard above their noise was the constant pop of champagne corks. It wasn't until several weeks later that I found out there were many such places all around the country that were celebrating our victory at the same time, and in much the same way.

The following day Mako told me to take the day off. I wasn't going to be competing in the Men's All-Around Finals (Peter and Mitch had won the honor, as had Bart who nudged me out of the all-important third place), so Mako told me to get some rest. He said I would need it. Boy, would I need it.

Telegrams and telephone calls were pouring in from all over the country. It was apparent there was no way I'd be able to rest in the Olympic Village, so I decided to go for a walk.

I walked through the streets of Westwood, and, unbelievably, people recognized me. I guess I was in a daze—I was surprised each time someone came up to me.

"Aren't you Tim Daggett?" they asked.

I smiled. Man, the muscles in my jaw were beginning to hurt.

I turned a corner to go down a side street, thinking maybe there would be no one around there. From out of nowhere a young Mexican woman approached me.

"You're one of the boys who won the gold medal last night," she said, beaming.

"Yes," I answered.

She looked at me with tears in her eyes. "I've been living in this country a few years now and I just became an American citizen," she spoke quietly. "When you won that medal you made me cry. For the first time, I know what it is like to feel proud to be an American."

I was overwhelmed.

I really wanted Peter to win the Men's All-Around title. I knew he had the best chance of all our guys, even though he was up against some tough competitors. I sat in the stands that night and watched the competition, feeling every emotion that Peter was feeling, I'm sure.

He put in a great performance, and after five events was running neck and neck for the gold with Japan's Koji Gushiken. China's Li Ning was not far behind, in third.

Peter's last event was the parallel bars. I had been keeping track and knew if he was able to score a 10 he would win. And I knew he could win, if he could just stick his dismount.

The crowd was screaming "Come on, Pete! Let's go, Pete!"

The noise faded a bit as he prepared for his routine. I stood up in my seat, shook my fist and shouted "Come on! Stick it, man!"

Peter turned and looked up into the stands. He caught my eye. I've no idea if he heard what I was saying, but I can still see the look he gave me. There was a little smile, but more than that, he seemed to say "I hear you, buddy. I hear you, man."

He mounted the bars and did a perfect performance, dismounted and landed . . . but he took a little hop. The smallest, most inconsequential hop. But he didn't stick.

I uttered an agonizing and highly audible groan. Peter ended up only .025 behind Gushiken and took the silver. Li Ning won the bronze.

I understood Peter's disappointment even better two nights later during the Men's Individual competition. Both of us had made the finals on the pommel horse for the United States. I was really nervous; I really wanted to win this one. In the past year and a half I had won every competition on the horse, so I knew my chances were good. But I came into the night with a 9.95 and a 9.9 from the first two nights of competition; Peter had a 10 and a 9.9. And Li Ning was going to be tough to beat.

Li was up first and did an awesome routine. He scored a 10. Some quick calculating told me there was no way I could get the gold. Then it was Peter's turn. He, too, did an awesome routine. He scored a 10. They were tied for the gold.

Man, was I discouraged. All I could hope for was the bronze. I'd like to say I got up there and did my best routine possible anyway, but I didn't. After the excitement of winning the team gold, this took the wind out of my sails. I *liked* being a gold winner, not a bronze. I did, however, do a decent routine, though it only scored a 9.9. I took the bronze.

As it turned out, Li had a great night. Though he had been disappointed in only taking the team silver, he certainly made up for it in the Individual competition, winning two golds and two silvers. What a great gymnast!

Meanwhile, the cards and letters kept pouring in with congratulatory messages from more people than I could ever have imagined: gym clubs from all over the country, congressmen, senators, governors and scores of people from "back home." They were sent to UCLA, the USGF, the Olympic Committee and West Springfield High School; and among them, one letter was miraculously delivered to my family's home, sent by an eight-year-old boy in the Midwest—addressed simply to "Tim Daggett—Olympic Gold Medalist": no street, no city, no state.

I wasn't able to see my family as often as I would have liked: it seemed there was always another interview, another appearance to be made. One night, however, we were able to meet for dinner—well, actually we went to Numero Uno Pizza, which was all we could afford!—and that's when I got my first real taste of what fame is all about: each time I left the Olympic Village from here on out I was escorted to the car by a security guard. I honestly didn't realize the impact of this until I was asked by Mobil Oil to do an appearance in New York City at a Big Apple Games clinic—a festival of about one thousand inner-city school-age athletes.

This was to take place while the Olympics were still going on; I had just enough time to sneak off to New York City, do the appearance, and fly back to Los Angeles for the closing ceremonies.

I was escorted to the Los Angeles airport, and when I got out of the car, suddenly, from out of nowhere, hundreds of people surrounded me.

"It's him!" they shouted.

"*U-S-A! U-S-A!*"

"Yea! Tim Daggett!"

"Can I have your autograph?"

They were all screaming at once, pushing and shoving one another, trying to squeeze their way through to get to me. Pens were waving in the air and arms were sticking through the masses, touching me on my arms, my shoulders, my back. I was totally freaked out. This was Los Angeles International Airport! I had been here countless times waiting for so many planes over the past few years and don't think I'd ever seen so many people!

Airport security quickly guided me through the crowd and took me to a private room in the terminal. I sat down, stunned. Where did they all come from? How did they know I was going to be there? To this day, it remains a mystery to me.

It was time to board the plane and one of the airline personnel came into the room.

"Mr. Daggett?" she asked.

Mr. Daggett? Was my father here? Oh, God. She was talking to *me*!

"Yes?" I tried to act cool.

"In order to prevent any further commotion, the airline has decided to move you up to first class, at no extra cost, of course. We'll board you after all passengers are on the plane. Is that all right with you?"

First class? Is that all right with me? This celebrity stuff wasn't too bad after all.

I smiled. I was cool. "Sure. That will be fine." Like this happens every day to me, right?

Somewhere over the Rockies, while I was gloating over lunch served on fine china with a linen napkin, a line of people started in the aisle. They were not, as I'd first suspected, waiting to use the rest room; they were waiting until I had finished eating to ask for my autograph. Everyone was so nice; they were really happy to see me. They asked about all the guys on the team; they asked what it was really like to beat the Chinese. It was the quickest, most enjoyable cross-country flight I'd ever taken.

By the time we landed in New York I was exhausted, and eager to get off the plane. At least in Kennedy Airport I knew there wouldn't be a mob scene. I walked unnoticed through the terminal to the entrance where a limousine was going to meet me. I stepped out onto the sidewalk, and stood there a moment to get my bearings. A Yellow Cab pulled up in front of me and slammed on the brakes.

The cabbie leaned across the seat and yelled to me out the window.

"Yea, Daggett! You're the guy who did it! All right!"

I was so startled I just smiled and nodded.

"Congratulations, kid!" He raised his arm. "U-S-A!" he shouted, then sped off, smiling.

Well, recognition in L.A. was one thing. New York City was another. To think a cabbie zooming down the street actually stopped and knew who I was, was just too much to take. I sat down on my gym bag and waited for the limo. Maybe we really had done something to lift the spirits of America. Wow! It was amazing.

Back in Los Angeles it was time for the closing ceremonies. So much had happened in the past two weeks, it was still a whirlwind in my mind. This time when we walked into the arena the crowd was even louder, bursting forth with raised decibels when they saw it was the U.S. Men's Gymnastics Team. It was so exciting. I was walking next to Peter and we tried to speak to each other but it was impossible to hear. So we just kept smiling with arms raised and backs straight and proud.

Toward the end of the ceremonies, during the magnificent fireworks display, I happened to glance up at the huge video screen, which was showing clips of outstanding performances throughout the Games. Suddenly, there I was, going through my high bar routine. What a thrill! Those ninety thousand people who had greeted us two weeks earlier were now cheering for me, and I couldn't stop the tears from rushing down my cheeks. The Games were over.

Then the tours began.

The first tour, sponsored by the Southland Corporation, was for all the Olympic medalists. It was a five-day, five-city tour, and had all the madcap excitement, adventure, and speed of touring ten European countries in ten days. There were receptions, parades, and more receptions, and it was more fun than any of us had had in years. We had, after all, spent the past year doing nothing much more than training for the Olympics. Now we were free!

We were told we could bring someone on tour with us, so I was on the phone to my brother Michael in an instant. I not only wanted to see him, I wanted him to have some of the fun! It was payback time, now that I finally had something I could share with my family after all they had sacrificed for me.

Michael met me in L.A., where the tour began. The first stop was Monday, August 13—breakfast with President and Mrs. Reagan. We all got to meet them and have our pictures taken with them. Imagine, me, meeting the President! They wouldn't believe this back in West Springfield!

Tuesday it was on to Washington D.C.; Wednesday, New York City. They had a real live ticker tape parade for us, which was spectacular!

That night I broke away from the tour group and flew up to Syracuse, where I had been asked to speak before sixteen thousand athletes and spectators at the opening ceremonies for the Empire State Games. I was in such a state of "cloud 9" that I never thought about getting nervous; in fact, I never thought about what I was going to say! I was to follow Governor Cuomo, who had just delivered an invigorating speech at the Democratic Convention and was now considered one of the hottest speakers around. When he introduced me and I stood up at the podium, the reception I got was unbelievable, absolute pandemonium! After they quieted down, I first asked them to please be patient with me.

"The only time I've gotten up in front of a group to speak was two semesters ago in a speech class," I admitted, then added, "and I didn't get an A."

The crowd roared with approval, and I was on a roll. I talked about the Olympics; I talked about commitment and dedication; I talked about the thrill of the Gold, my words coming in a rush from the incredible glory ride I was on. The people loved it. And, for the first time, I discovered how much fun public speaking could be.

Michael and I were scheduled to rejoin the tour in Orlando the following morning. My friends and fellow gymnasts from UCLA, Mark and Chris Caso, were from Syracuse, and Chris was home. We went to his house after my speech for a much-needed break. This celebrity stuff was exciting, but now everywhere we went I was recognized. It felt good to sit in the kitchen of a friend, have a cup of coffee, put my feet up on the chair and be myself.

Chris stirred his coffee and looked at me across the table.

"Tim," he said, "do you understand what's happened?"

"Well, sort of," I answered, then laughed. "It's such a blur right now!" I stared down at my coffee.

Chris laughed. "You guys are *huge*, man! You guys are *stars!*"

Stars? It took Chris to say it, but his words really sank in. He was right. Now, for the moment, anyway, we were stars. It was weird.

The next morning Michael and I took off for Orlando. Having to make connections in New York City from Syracuse, by the time we arrived in Florida it was too late to make the reception; we waited at the airport for the other medalists to return; then it was off to Dallas for more celebrations on Friday.

Throughout the tour we checked in at home several times, and each time, my mom kept saying the same thing:

"You've got to be here Saturday, Tim. There's going to be a party for you."

We were able to arrange reservations and plane tickets, and finally assured her we would be there. We would be arriving at my old home base, Bradley International Airport, at 2:30 P.M. She was a little vague about what exactly she meant by "a party," but I figured my family and some of my old friends maybe were getting together for a quiet little celebration.

Nothing could have been further from the truth.

10

By now I was becoming accustomed to being the last one off the plane: last one on, last one off was the way the airlines usually preferred it for crowd control. I still didn't know how people knew I was on the plane.

We landed at Bradley, and Michael and I stayed in our seats, waiting for instructions from the flight attendant. After all the other passengers were off, she finally came to us and said, "Welcome home, Tim. You can leave now."

"Welcome home, Tim." Hey, that was really nice of her. Somehow, she knew this was home.

We walked toward the gate and I was only vaguely aware of the sounds of a crowd: it was one noise I was getting used to. I couldn't wait to see my family and to prove to Mom that I indeed had made it home and that I wore the red Olympic blazer and white duck pants she'd asked me to wear.

As we got to the gate I could see her standing there, waving and smiling. Beside her were my uncle, my grandparents, and I could see the tops of the heads of some of the kids behind them. We were about six feet away from the welcoming hugs when the sound of trumpets filled the air, then flourished into a full-fledged band. I reached Mom and hugged her, then looked up and saw an unbelievable crowd, waving, cheering, holding up signs that read WELCOME HOME, TIM. Off to the side was the West Springfield High School Alumni Band, led by, who else, my old band director, Mr. DiGiore. They were playing the Olympic theme song.

Wow. If I'd thought anything before had been overwhelming, I obviously couldn't have imagined this. There were TV cameras everywhere, scanning so many familiar and so many new faces. We were escorted out to the front of the terminal, into the August sunshine.

"We have to wait here a minute," Mom told us. "There's going to be a motorcade back to town."

A *motorcade?*

They planted me atop the backseat of a Cadillac convertible; Michael, Mom, and Coach Jones climbed into the car, and we left the airport, with a police escort, to thread our way along nearly twenty miles of back roads north to West Springfield. All along the way people were lined up with signs and banners, and lots of applause. It was wonderful.

"The newspaper published the parade route in today's paper," Mom shouted back to me, when I asked where all the people had come from.

"The Springfield newspaper?" I asked.

"Front page," she answered proudly.

Wow, I thought. Wow. That was all I could seem to say.

As we approached the Vietnam Veterans' Bridge leading in to town, I noticed that the crowd had grown still larger, and there were fire trucks parked across from each other on the bridge. They sounded their sirens and I looked up to see the enormous "snorkel" ladder arching its way across the bridge where it connected with the ladder from another fire truck. From this arch hung a huge banner, framed by two American flags. The banner read WELCOME HOME, TIM.

Just past the bridge our motorcade was met by a group of antique cars which tagged along the back of the parade, and we headed for the center of town, traveling slowly down those wonderful streets of home, streets with names depicting the great New England small town this is: Church Street (past the old "Y"), Westfield Street, Elm Street to Park Avenue to Memorial Avenue.

All along the route were thousands and thousands of people, with countless kids waving American flags.

"The Rotary and the Chamber of Commerce donated the money for the flags," Mom explained.

"There are four thousand of them!" Coach Jones added. It turned out that Bill Shepard, one of the local pharmacists, had to engage the help of the town's Boy Scouts and Girl Scouts in distributing the flags to the kids all along the route.

Beyond the faces, the flags and the clicking cameras I could see the signs—every conceivable type of hand-painted sign and banner hung from the front porches and storefront businesses that line the shady streets: WELCOME HOME, GOLDEN BOY! TIM—YOU'RE A PERFECT 10! CONGRATULATIONS, TIM DAGGETT!

As we reached Elm Street I noticed an apartment building under construction—across the framed front of the three-story building was painted an enormous sign: TIM DAGGETT—WEST SIDE'S PRIDE. There were people standing on top of the building and I could no longer hold in my enthusiasm. I asked the driver to stop the car, and I leaped out of the back, and raced up the makeshift stairs to the top of the building, shaking hands and saying "thank you" over and over. "Thank you" seemed so inadequate compared with what my feelings really were. I just could not believe my town had done this for me, and more than that, I couldn't believe all these people were there for me!

At four o'clock we arrived at the grounds of the Eastern States Exposition—"The Big E," New England's great state fair where every kid from West Springfield spent every growing-up year each fall—and were directed through the crowds to the "Court of Flags" for the ceremonies.

I went up to the platform and stood looking out at the crowd—there were twenty-five hundred people there alone! There were more flags and signs and tons of red, white and blue balloons which said *Tim Daggett Days*. But one thing in particular caught my eye, and I started to laugh. There, high above the others, was one sign, artfully printed in bold letters: AREN'T YOU GLAD WE MADE YOU EAT YOUR VEGGIES? Through the faces I recognized that of the woman holding the sign— she had been one of the cafeteria workers at my elementary school.

The band was playing; the high school cheerleaders were performing, and I was thrilled beyond belief.

Town Selectman Chairman J. Edward Christian presented me with a key to the town and thanked me for being "a shining light for generations to come."

I then received mementos and citations from U.S. Congressman Silvio Conte, State Department of Commerce Regional Director Peter Lappin, Hampden County Commission Chairman Thomas O'Connor, State Representative Linda Melconian and State Representative Walter DeFilippi, who also presented a citation to Coach Jones.

Then came the most meaningful reward of my career. It was announced that the high school gymnasium where I had practiced was being named the Timothy Daggett Gymnasium. That one brought tears to my eyes, and I didn't dare look over at Coach Jones.

The president of the Lions Club, James Martin, presented me with the banners to be hung in the gym; then the town postmaster, Raymond Sbalbi, gave me a commemorative issue of "Golden Moments"—stamps which had been issued especially for the Olympics.

Dr. Frederick S. Conlin, a town selectman and cochairman of this welcoming committee with Thomas F. "Jinx" Powers, then gave a brief description of my gymnastics career leading up to the Olympics. Then the tough part: I was introduced, and I knew I had to stand up and "say a few words."

While the crowd was applauding, my thoughts were racing. What on earth was I going to say? How could I ever say "thank you" to all these people who had turned out to congratulate me? What could I say that could possibly make them understand how much this meant to me?

The applause died down and I thought, *Well, Daggett, you'd better think fast*. Mom was smiling beside me—she knew I'd think of something!

First, I thanked my family. Then, I thanked Coach Jones. I wanted the world to know my gratitude for their support over the years, and it seemed that telling all of West Springfield was a good place to begin. I talked a little bit about the thrill of the Olympics, and, in trying to thank all these people, I finally knew what to say.

"I've traveled around the world over the past few years, and in the past few weeks have traveled the country, receiving congratulations and wonderful receptions at every stop." I paused, looked around at the smiling crowd, then, with the deep sincerity I truly felt, I added, "But as Dorothy said in *The Wizard of Oz* . . . there really is, no place like home."

"Some 'party'!" I said to my family later, when I was sprawled out on the living room floor.

They all kind of looked at me and laughed. Then Mom spoke up.

"It's not over," she said.

"What do you mean?" I looked at her suspiciously.

"There's more tomorrow."

"Tomorrow?"

"There's a banquet tomorrow."

"A banquet?"

"Yes. Oh, and you have to plant a tree."

"Plant a tree?"

"On the town green."

This was too much. Later, as I lay in bed I couldn't help but think of Peter. Peter's "hometown" was Los Angeles, and he had mentioned that he had gone to meet the mayor. He could have no conception of what it was like to come from a small town that really cared about its "heroes." I was so grateful, almost embarrassed over all this fuss for me. But it was through all this that I realized how much my "10" had meant to the people of West Springfield. It seemed to have brought them together in the true spirit of small-town New England, joined them together if only for a short while, to share in a little excitement and to make them feel proud. As I went to sleep that night my embarrassment lifted, and I was filled with the good feelings that only come when you share of yourself.

The next morning was overcast, and there was a threat of rain.

"This will probably keep the crowds away," Mom commented.

But when we got to the town green at twelve-thirty, they were there: hundreds of them, thousands. I was to plant a red oak tree, a gift from the Massachusetts Tree Wardens and Foresters Association, in front of the white wood gazebo. West Springfield tree warden Seth Swift said the tree was selected "to typify Tim and his many attributes." He said the tree "is a symbol of grandeur, strength and durability . . . prized for its noble aspect, vigorous upright growth and seasonal coloration . . . of hardy northern stock, of great longevity, and well adapted to its surroundings."

After the tree was planted, I went up to the gazebo with the committee cochairman Mr. Powers, who announced that all kids in the audience were welcome to come up and shake my hand. This, for me, was the best part, to see the smiles on the faces of the kids, to see their eyes light up when I asked their names. I could see in them the importance of heroes, and I knew then that I would always do everything possible to live up to their image; but beyond that, I wanted them to see me as a person—just another guy from West Springfield, who had done something not unlike anything they could do.

Years later when I heard John Naber, the Olympic swimmer, say "Olympic champions aren't extraordinary people; they're ordinary people who have accomplished extraordinary things," I thought of this first encounter of mine with the kids in the gazebo. I couldn't have said it better.

My entire family was then packed up in a motorcade again and escorted to the historic Storrowtown Carriage House, where the luncheon was to be held. The restaurant was sold out—over seven hundred people had bought tickets to be there. I was really humbled when I saw that Bishop McGuire was joining us at the head table; and, again, when U.S. Representative Edward Boland presented me with the American flag that had flown over the Capitol on July 31—the day I got the "10". He then presented another flag—this one had flown over the Capitol the day before, the eighteenth of August, the day I returned to town—to the Board of Selectmen.

After lunch more people came up to greet me, but I was disappointed. While I could see old friends lingering in the background, those who hovered around me were mostly people I hadn't known before. Why weren't my friends coming up to me? I wanted to shout "John, get over here! Maria! Cindy! Come here!" But I knew that wouldn't be appropriate, and I watched many of my friends duck out the door without ever having said "Hi." That was really upsetting. Did they think I had changed? Did they think that—of all people—I wouldn't want to share these moments with them? Those questions stayed with me for a long time. My friends were always so important to me, and they still are. It hurt me that they might think they weren't wanted.

We left the restaurant to go out to the grounds, where yet another ceremony was about to begin. It was drizzling now, but the people were prepared: amid American flags and "Tim Daggett Days" balloons were hundreds of umbrellas, shielding well-wishers from the unpredictable New England weather.

Bernard Crosby, controller for the Springfield newspapers and a West Springfield townsman, presented me with the full-page coverage of the "Homecoming Events" from the newspaper; then Ray Hershel, news director for one of the local television stations, played a videotape on a large screen for all to see—a compilation of clips of my Olympic performances, plus of many performances never before seen. He also announced that in a couple of weeks, this tape, as well as tape taken during these two days, would be aired in a half-hour television program. The selectmen then announced that there would be a street named in my honor: "Tim Daggett Drive," which would be dedicated "as soon as a new street came into being"!

I was exhausted from the weekend's activities. I was tired of smiling, but I didn't want it to stop. I was so proud to have been raised in a town such as West Springfield, and still so overwhelmed at all they had done for me. There really was "no place like home," and I was filled with gratitude.

11

Being home always had a way of bringing me back to reality, to where I wanted to be. Home was a safety net for me . . . the one place I knew I could count on to renew my strength of spirit and togetherness of soul.

After the "homecoming" I flew to New York City for a press conference. By now the cameras were familiar to me, and I was becoming more and more conscious of my appearance. Ever since I was a kid I'd had one eyetooth that protruded a little. It never bothered me before, but now each time I saw a picture of myself the image of that tooth screamed at me.

"This is ugly!" it said. "It makes you look like a jerk."

Without realizing it, I decided to turn Hollywood. If my face was going to be plastered everywhere, I wanted it to look great. And I needed it to look great *fast*.

Armed with the inflated ego of being in the limelight, I hotfooted it to a dentist in the city.

"Yes, I can help you," he said convincingly. "Yes, I can correct the problem quickly."

"Quickly" sounded much better than the year or two of wearing braces or a retainer my dentist back home had recommended.

The dentist applied some bonding material not only to my eyetooth, but also to all my other front teeth to "even them off," he said. "The camera will only see your smile as a whole, and it will project a look of continuity."

"Doesn't this mean all my front teeth will protrude?" I asked.

"Not to the camera," he said, "and the camera is what should be important to you now. Give it a little time and you'll get used to it."

I left his office feeling as though I was wearing a mouth guard, which would have been great if I was about to go onto the football field or hockey rink. Such was the price of fame, I rationalized. The camera had become my future; vanity had become my allegiance.

Armed with my new smile and superficial confidence, I went from the city to spend a few days at a gymnastics camp in upstate New York to "rest up" and get ready for the next influx of tours. Everything was going great until I met the first group of young kids.

Their little faces glowed when they saw me, and their eyes sparkled with excitement.

"Hi, Tim!" they said, one after another.

I tried to smile back and found I just couldn't. Something stopped me. It was my damned teeth! Being with the kids made me self-conscious; I didn't want them to think I was trying to be someone I wasn't; I didn't want them to think I had compromised myself for publicity.

For four days I stayed at the camp, talking with countless kids and signing as many autographs. I never smiled; I just grinned a closed-mouth grin and must have seemed pretty unfriendly. It was awful. Before I left the camp I went to a dentist up there and had the bonding material removed. Cameras be damned; I was going to be myself.

Then it was off to Chicago, back home and on to Boston for a *Sports Illustrated* banquet. In between we were able to sneak one day for ourselves, and Peter and Mitch came back to West Springfield with me to see my family and to, at long last, meet the infamous Big Mac.

Several times over the past few years I had entertained the guys in the gym with my tales of Big Mac's talents.

"I can't believe it!" Peter screamed as we watched Big Mac perform. "He looks just like you!"

"Not really," I said. "Look, his ears are pointed."

"No, man, I mean he looks just like you do when you imitate him! He really does everything you said!"

Well, of course he does! Did they honestly not believe my Doberman was trained to sit at the table and answer the phone? I tell you, these L.A. boys have a lot to learn about Yankee smarts.

After the *Sports Illustrated* banquet I was off to Sea World in San Diego where I did the exhibition with U.S. Women's Gold medalist Julianne McNamara.

The exhibition was outside. We were using unfamiliar equipment and didn't have time to warm up properly, which is no excuse for what happened to me but it makes it sound better. There were hundreds of people in the audience, and they were excited to see us. But their applause turned to hysterical laughter when, after a seemingly brilliant performance on the parallel bars, I did a magnificent dismount, went very high in the air, and landed squarely in the geraniums.

I stood up with red blossoms stuck to my shirt.

"This is a demonstration of the importance of creativity in gymnastics," I said to the crowd, and they laughed all the more.

I had my picture taken with Sea World's celebrated black and white whale Shamu (I smiled!) and was off once again, this time to Florida for an exhibition and speaking engagement for General Development Corporation.

There were hundreds of kids there, and when I walked out onto the stage I got an incredible chill. Every one of the kids had on an identical T-shirt made especially for the event—and each T-shirt had my autograph scrawled across the front in big, bold letters. It was pretty awesome. Though I was aware that my life had changed because of the Olympics, this kind of reminder was always sneaking up on me, taking me off guard, exposing me as a celebrity. It was a humbling experience.

I returned home to West Springfield where I received the Rotary's prestigious Paul Harris Fellowship Award; then it was on to Boston for yet another parade and celebration. It had only been one month since the closing ceremonies of the Olympic Games, and it seemed like a century. My world had gone from the relative quiet of a gym to the hum of the inside of an airplane and the deafening sounds of cheering people.

On September 14 the team was back together again for McDonald's Gold Medalist Tour—with appearances in Washington, D.C., Houston, Albuquerque and Indianapolis. There was one day between Albuquerque and Indianapolis: Mitch, Bart and I flew to Michigan for an appearance at a shopping mall. That was a scary one. No one, including mall security personnel, had anticipated the huge crowd we would draw—a huge *and* overly enthusiastic crowd! We signed autographs for hours amid people pushing, shouting and being totally unruly. Finally they managed to get us away from what had turned into a mob scene. It was not a pleasant experience.

When the tour was over I was off to Maine, then back to L.A., back to New York, back to L.A., back to New York. The offers kept pouring in, and during one week I took the "red-eye" from New York to Los Angeles three times. And, unlike the other guys on the team, I had not retired from gymnastics. Which meant I still had to find places to work out.

On one "jaunt" I flew from Los Angeles for a morning photo session in New York. When that was finished, I had a few hours to kill before my scheduled interviews at all three network affiliates. I grabbed a cab to the airport and hopped a shuttle to New Haven, where I worked out in the Southern Connecticut State University gym; then jumped another shuttle back to the city, made it just in time for the interviews; then flew back to Los Angeles. It was exhausting, and I was quickly becoming addicted to coffee. But it was all so exciting!

In fact, it was either that night or one of those many nights that I was thrilled to meet one of my favorite actors.

I was sitting in first class (this was one of the best parts of "celebritydom"), waiting for the rest of the passengers to board. When the plane was nearly full, suddenly one guy appeared beside me. I glanced up quickly and noticed he had a beard, baseball cap and about a three days' growth of whiskers. I didn't look at him long enough to recognize his face as he tried to stuff his duffle bag in the compartment over my head.

"Oh, no," I thought. "This guy is going to be a problem."

As he crammed the bag into the compartment, part of it drooped down in my face. I saw the scribbled words on a piece of tape stuck to the side of the bag: *W. Murray. Ghostbuster Lane.* I thought, oh, brother, this guy's a winner. He finally managed to get his bag in, and he sat down across the aisle. Suddenly it dawned on me! It actually was *Bill Murray!* I was dying to meet him, but I didn't want to seem "uncool," so I thought I'd wait until we were airborne. But as soon as that happened, a line of kids appeared out of nowhere.

"Can we have your autograph?" they asked me—one after another after another. I started signing the back of airline ticket folders, airline napkins and crumpled pieces of paper. At one point I looked up and caught Bill Murray's eye. He was watching it all, smiling, and he gave me the thumbs up. After my "fans" went back to their seats, Bill struck up a conversation.

"So how does it feel, man?" he asked with a smile. "Last month you couldn't even get a parking space in Westwood and now you're a big star!"

We talked for a while about "the price of fame" and I really got a kick out of him. He is as funny in person as he is on the screen, and he certainly made that trip go fast!

The hectic pace continued in city after city: giving exhibitions, making speeches, promoting the next tour stops. One day I actually was able to grab some time and fly to Pennsylvania to stop in at Woodward Gymnastics Camp. I had a good workout, saw many of my friends, and was scheduled to fly out early the next morning. That night I went to the neighborhood hangout with some of the guys. There was a television set over the bar and "The Tonight Show" was on. I was half watching it, when, out of the corner of my eye, a familiar face came on it. It was Peter. What a weird feeling, sitting in a bar across the country with just a bunch of "regular" guys and suddenly seeing your best friend sitting in that famous chair beside Johnny Carson's desk. It was another one of those little incidents which quickly jolted me back to the reality of all that had happened.

The most difficult part of all the appearances was lack of time. It bothered me that at most of the exhibitions there simply wasn't time to sign autographs. The fact that the crowds took the trouble to come out and see us certainly merited the signing of autographs . . . but it was always rush, rush, rush! After the exhibitions we quickly showered, grabbed some dinner and left the arena to board the buses . . . there were people still waiting for us, hoping we could squeeze in a few minutes to sign their programs. Some actually followed the buses to our hotel, and we had to shut off our phones. It didn't seem fair, but there just wasn't enough time!

Pittsburgh, Hartford, Los Angeles, Chicago, Philadelphia, Boston, Atlanta, Cincinnati, New York City—my calendar was beginning to look like a timetable for the airlines. Each time I flew into a new city I immediately called the press.

"I'm here," I told them. "I can give you about an hour for an interview."

They came in droves, in the small towns and big cities alike. We were news; we were hot. And by making ourselves accessible to the media we created great public relations for keeping the spirit of the Olympics alive, and for generating momentous enthusiasm for the sport of gymnastics.

As we made it into November, it was time for yet another new experience: we were going to be guests on an episode of the television show "Different Strokes." It took a full five days to complete: three days of rehearsals, one run-through, and one day of actual shooting.

Just being at the studio was as exciting as doing the program. Everywhere we went there were movie stars upon movie stars, and they all recognized us! We liked to think it was because of our "fame," when in actuality it was probably because six guys—six short guys—walking together certainly set us apart from the crowd. Our red, white, and blue warm-up suits with "U-S-A" boldly across our backs may have given them a clue, too!

At one point on the studio grounds Peter, Mitch, and I noticed an absolutely gorgeous woman getting into a white Rolls Royce. We recognized her as actress Kelly LeBrock, who was there filming the movie *Weird Science*. Wow, what a knockout! It was when we went over to the car that I noticed her two beautiful Dobermans.

"Whoa!" I cried. "Check out the dogs!" I think we hurt her feelings when we turned our attention to them, but I could relate better to a Doberman than to a glamorous movie star!

I was looking forward to Thanksgiving. I was scheduled to appear in the Macy's parade, and that meant I wouldn't be too far from West Springfield. I flew to Boston for an appearance on Sunday the eighteenth, and left there for home—where I would actually have a full week before I had to be anywhere else but the parade!

My brother David went to the parade with me, and it was freezing. In fact, it stands out in memory as the day of my life when I was the coldest I had ever been and, hopefully, would ever be again.

I was on a McDonald's float with Mary Lou Retton and a number of other sports stars from the United States. I wore my McDonald's sweatsuit and wished I had three others underneath it. I had never realized how much colder the wind is when it whips through the openings between tall skyscrapers.

"Gee, Tim, this is really fun," David said through chattering teeth when I met him after the parade. "I never thought winning the gold could be this invigorating."

We couldn't wait to get home to Mom's turkey and stuffing. *Hot* turkey and stuffing.

I guess it was while I was home for Thanksgiving that I started thinking about where my life was headed. I left there a little depressed as I boarded yet another plane—this time for Georgia, then on to Jackson, Mississippi. Over the next week I took a long, hard look at myself and my life. The nonstop breakfasts, luncheons, and dinners were beginning to show on my waistline. In the four months since the Olympics I had rarely been in a gym, and what little workout I managed to get doing exhibitions simply wasn't anything like training; it was just fooling around. Combined with it all, I was exhausted.

I returned home a couple of weeks into December, wanting to do nothing more than sleep. Yet I awoke each morning feeling even more tired. That's when I realized something was missing from my life. For thirteen years I had had a dream—every day I had known what I was going to do to make that dream come true. Suddenly, I had no focus, no reason to charge me up and get me through the day. Now, I didn't even have to get out of bed if I didn't want to.

I had no idea what to do with my life. Should I go back into training? Financially, that would be a pretty stupid move. Now was the time to capitalize on the fame—who knew how long it would last? After making so many sacrifices for so many years, it seemed ludicrous that I could even think about going back to gymnastics. There was money in fame: there was no money in being an amateur athlete. Did I really want to spend the rest of my life wondering how I was going to buy my next car or if I'd have enough money to fly home when I wanted to?

But those long mornings trying to force myself to get out of bed told me something I guess I already knew: while the bright lights and the fans were a kick, it simply wasn't me.

I decided to try and train for a day, just one day, to see how it felt. Well, I'd been right about one thing—I certainly was out of shape. I struggled through the workout like a slug. Working out for four hours had always been a piece of cake compared with the even greater rigors of training. Now it was all I could do to get through a simple workout. But when the day was over, aching and tired as I was, I felt good. I felt good on the inside, because I was where I belonged—in a gym—and because I was doing what came so naturally to me—I was struggling.

That night I decided to go back into training. Enough of the glitz and the glamour. I wanted—no, I *needed*—gymnastics to feel fulfilled. Plus, I still had that little matter of an education to complete. I had reduced my classes to a minimum in preparation for the Olympics, so I still had a year left to go to obtain my degree.

It seemed a bit crazy—it was only a little over a week until Christmas and I'd want to be home for that, but I didn't want to wait until after the holidays: I knew that once I had made the decision, I had to act. Not tomorrow, not next week or next month. If I was going to do this, I was going to do it now.

Not waiting for the inevitable opportunity to be flown back to the West Coast at the expense of a tour sponsor or private company for an exhibition or speech, I dusted off my MasterCard and bought a one-way ticket.

The next day, I flew to Los Angeles and went back to the gym.

12

When I returned to L.A. and announced I was going back into training, the reactions I received were surprisingly disappointing, and included a host of discouragements from "Why bother?" to "Why would you even want to try?" But I was only twenty-two—I had been the youngest member of the 1984 team, and I was not yet ready to give up the sport I loved. Little did I know it was never to be the same again.

Things were different: Mako was gone, and I had a new coach, Yefim Furman, a former gymnast from the Soviet Union; Peter and Mitch were gone, both having retired after the Olympics; I would no longer be competing for UCLA because NCAA rules allow competition for only four years; I had gone from being the youngest team member to the oldest and the most experienced; and, I was now a celebrity, and for the first time in my life, there was the opportunity for me to earn money.

Well, okay, I thought. So things are different. I'm not different, am I? I'm still Tim Daggett, the same goofy kid who started selling shamrocks on street corners at the age of seven and made it through that first summer in L.A. on twenty dollars; the same competitive, headstrong kid who bulled his way beyond talent and experience to make the Olympic team. I can become a champion once again. It may seem like starting all over, but I can do it. I can do it.

Whoever said that some things are easier said than done must have had me in mind. Whether it was from innocence or pure pigheadedness, I really wasn't prepared for the changes in my life.

Mako had left UCLA for a coaching position in Australia. After training with him for four years, I had become accustomed to his methods of training: "Train long and train hard. Harder than the other guy," was Mako's philosophy.

Yefim, on the other hand, was a more technically oriented coach, who insisted that I change the way I performed certain skills in order to get them right.

Where Mako was more inclined to instill in me the need for practice, practice, practice, Yefim said, "First get it right. Then we practice, practice."

Changing the way I performed each skill was most difficult and time-consuming, yet Yefim brought to my training a whole new perspective. I'm still not sure which of their two methods is the best, maybe a little of both. I do know that between the "changing" and the "practicing" that had been drilled into my head, I began training harder than even I thought possible.

I had first met Yefim in my early years at UCLA. He was coaching at a private club in L.A., which had the luxury of something we didn't have in the old UCLA gym—a tumbling pit. A couple of times a week we went to the club with Mako and took advantage of the "pit" for learning new skills. It was much easier on the bones to attempt triple back flips off the rings and land in a cushioned pit rather than landing on a four-inch-thick landing mat.

While we worked out there, I watched Yefim and liked his style. He was different from Mako, no doubt about it. I knew he had tremendous knowledge—he had been a top gymnast in the Soviet Union, and his experience was vast. When Mako left UCLA I suggested to Art Shurlock, the head gymnastics coach, that Yefim be given the position and, thankfully, Yefim was hired. The thought of starting over again was pretty scary, but if Yefim had been a total unknown it would have been terrifying.

So here I was with a new coach and without the stimulation of working with Peter and Mitch. Yup, this sure was going to be different. But never once did I doubt my decision.

Mark and Chris Caso were still training at UCLA, as was Robbie Campbell, another gymnast who had been on the UCLA team with me. At least there were some familiar faces! One of the freshman UCLA gymnasts brought with him not only a familiar face but also a touch of home: Curtis Holdsworth was from Wilbraham, Massachusetts (two towns east of West Springfield), and had, for the past two years, trained under Coach Jones.

The first emotion I felt when back in the gym was loneliness. I no longer had other guys to watch and to learn from: the others were watching me, looking to me for advice and expertise, even looking up to me. I felt the pressure of my Olympic success even now in the gym because the others thought I must have "all the answers." But who was going to give *me* the answers? Or at least blunder their way through alongside me? I didn't realize how dependent I'd become on Peter and Mitch: when you train together you grow together and your dreams and your goals become one. Now I was on my own, and without their interaction I had to shift from a team spirit to striving for individual success. Nothing stays the same.

Even the atmosphere in the gym had changed. Few people, if any, had bothered to come by and watch us train for 1984, and the all but behind-the-scenes sport of gymnastics was certainly nothing people sought out. Now, people actually lined up at the windows of the gym, peeking in and often shouting cheers.

"Yea, Tim!" The voices were muffled through the glass.

"Let's see the high bar routine!"

"Show us some flairs!"

It was unnerving. I couldn't go out and get a drink of water without being asked for my autograph. All I wanted to do was train, but if I'd ever had any delusions that I was leaving "celebrityville" behind me, I was dead wrong. Somehow I had to learn to strike a balance. I wanted my space but I didn't want to disappoint the "fans"! I still had a hard time believing people wanted my autograph in the first place, let alone wanted to spend their time hanging around a sweaty gym for the sole purpose of seeing me. But I think it was actually more than that. I think that what we accomplished at the 1984 Games brought gymnastics into a new light, and helped catapult it into the exciting spectator sport that it really is. As much as I had become a star, so had gymnastics, and for that I was glad.

Just as I was getting back into the swing of things, it was time for more appearances. With the holidays behind us and 1985 now flipped onto the calendars, I was back on the road, squeezing in a quick tour here, an exhibition there, trying, at least, to keep solvent. Because I wouldn't re-enroll in school until fall, there was no scholarship for me now: I was financially on my own.

Unfortunately each appearance, even if it was only for a day, took me away from the gym and broke the continuity of my training. I tried to keep them to a minimum, but some were too good to pass up.

One of the most fun times I've had was when the team was asked to perform for ABC's "Night of 100 Stars" in February. We were all back together (everyone but Bart, who'd had a prior commitment) and we had a great time. The show was produced at Radio City Music Hall in New York City, and we were surrounded by more jewels and furs than I'd ever imagined. They dressed us in silver-star-studded white uniforms (which were a bit much!) and we did a charged-up, choreographed routine along with the Pointer Sisters singing their hit song "Jump."

Being around so many famous people in one place was exciting. There was a huge poster that we had each been asked to sign, and I stood in line in front of Gregory Peck. What a thrill! The young guy ahead of me was a newcomer to show business, and when it came time for him to autograph the poster, he scrawled his name in huge bold letters, covering many names of much more famous people. I must have made a face at that, for Mr. Peck tapped me on the shoulder.

"The bigger the autograph, the smaller the star," he said with a smile. I immediately added my signature as small as possible, still having it legible. I didn't want Mr. Peck to think I was overly impressed with myself.

The show was an entirely new experience. For the first time, I saw a man wearing a fur coat—in fact, everyone there seemed to be wearing furs. I wondered how many months' rent I could pay on my apartment for the cost of one of them! I roomed next to Tony Danza, and felt totally out of my element. After the show, Peter and I were hanging around backstage and we met Matt Dillon.

"God, he's just like himself!" I said to Peter. "He's exactly like he is in the movies!"

"What did you expect?" Peter laughed. "We're all just *people*. Isn't that what you keep telling me?"

I had to laugh at that one. As much as I wanted others to think of me not as a celebrity but as Tim Daggett, small-town boy, it never dawned on me that bigger stars with greater exposure might also just be small-town boys at heart. I always figured they must be on some kind of untouchable pedestal . . . not unlike the way our fans often perceived us.

My first meet after the Olympics was the McDonald's American Cup in March, the largest international competition we have in this country. Although my training had been interrupted several times by public appearances, I somehow managed to win the meet, but not without yet another embarrassing moment. One thing about gymnastics, when you salute the judge and you're alone on the floor, all eyes are on you. It's not like in so many other sports where the audience is watching an entire team: there, if you screw up, you can always convince yourself that maybe the people were watching someone else while you quickly regain your composure.

My moment happened even before I mounted the first apparatus. After performing in over fifty tours since the Olympics, I had become adjusted to the hype of the crowds. In those exhibitions, the same thing always happens: the music swells to a crescendo; spotlights crisscross your body with disco precision; the enthusiastic announcer blares into the microphone:

"And now our next performer, Tim 'The Bull' Daggett . . . [the crowd explodes in applause] . . . Tim is best remembered for his exciting perfect 10 performance . . ." and on and on, at which point it was my cue to turn to the audience, wave vigorously with both arms and, above all, smile. Smile as big as I could. It was part of the show, part of what they had come to see.

Now, here I was at the American Cup, and it was my turn. I stood on the podium and heard the announcer.

"And now, Tim Daggett for the U.S.A."

Without thinking, I turned to the crowd and began to wave, my smile as broad as I had been trained by the public relations specialists. But there was no music, there were no spotlights, and the crowd looked at me as if I had lost my marbles. I quickly turned back to the judge, saluted, and got through my routine, with the proverbial egg still visible on my face.

I had three months after that to prepare for the U.S.A. Championships—the first qualifying meet for the 1985 World Championships, to be held in November in Montreal.

During those months I'd like to say I trained hard and trained well. I did not. Instead, I kept leaving the gym, flying off for another speech or exhibition. I performed an exhibition for ESPN; I did an NBC special from Caesar's Palace; I did an appearance on the "Merv Griffin Show." By the time June arrived I was only in half-great shape. I should have won that meet, but I ended up third. What made matters worse was I knew that the year before this could never have happened. I had lost my focus.

My mother had come to the meet along with my sister Susan, and Scott, who was now her husband. After the meet they talked seriously to me.

"Tim, maybe you should think about retiring," Scott said. "You could get hurt if you keep going on like this."

"Like what?" I asked, but I already knew the answer.

"Like you're only going through the motions. You just don't look like the same gymnast out there."

"Timmy, your dream has already come true," Susan added. "It's never going to be the same again."

Time for another long talk with myself. Deep down I knew the problem was not my lack of desire but my lack of money.

First, it was easy to blame the system. In 1985 the country's top gymnasts did not receive any compensation for living expenses, and were entitled to only a portion of what they were able to earn. I wasn't looking to get rich, but I did have to earn a living, to pay for my apartment, put gas in my car and English muffins and peanut butter on my table. I could not resist the temptation of giving one little talk or performing in one little exhibition if I could make money. How badly could it hurt my training? As unfair as I felt the system was, I learned that it's always easier to blame an unknown "force" rather than turn toward yourself as the reason for failure.

I knew there wasn't much I could do about changing the system, and I knew I sure didn't like coming in third. I also knew Scott and Susan were wrong: this was no time to think about retiring. But what they said jarred me back to reality. Money, alas, is not everything, and it sure didn't beat my feeling good about myself. I gave up touring and concentrated on training.

That August, Peter's wife gave birth to their first child, a son. When Peter called me to share their happy news, I was shaken by his words.

"We've decided to name him Timothy," he said.

"Why on earth would you want to name your kid *that*?" I laughed, but, for once, Peter didn't laugh back.

"Because we wanted to name him after someone special—someone who has the kind of qualities we hope he'll have someday; someone he can look to when he's older and say 'Hey, I was named after him!' and feel proud."

I was speechless.

"And we want him to follow your example. So that someday we can say to him 'Tim Daggett never compromised. And neither should you.' "

I choked up, unable to talk. Then Peter said the words which meant more than anything in the world to me.

"If this little guy grows up to be just like Tim Daggett, I'll be one happy dad."

At the final trials, I won the gold.

I went back to classes to complete my senior year, and started training for the World Championships. But, unbelievably, I still hadn't learned from my past mistakes, and picked up once again where I had left off—touring and speaking whenever the opportunity arose. Working out was often squeezed in at unfamiliar gyms in unknown towns; studying was done mostly on airplanes, not now while traveling to competitions but more often while en route to yet another speaking engagement. Though I should have won at least one medal at the World Championships, I was beginning to have my doubts.

Besides my lack of serious training, I felt another lack: the USA team simply wasn't the 1984 Olympic team. Although Scott Johnson had by now returned to gymnastics and had made the team, the others were inexperienced, younger guys. We didn't have the same spark, the same cohesiveness as we'd had in '84. Why should we? Peter, Mitch and I—we'd kind of grown up together. Though I'd competed with these "new" guys in years gone past, we didn't really know what made each other click. It was frustrating. I kept trying to find the spirit, trying to get together the "teamwork" that had come so naturally to our '84 team. I felt as much a cheerleader as a competitor. I was a fish out of water without Peter, Mitch and the others.

One of our guys—Phil Cahoy—fell the wrong way on the high bar during the compulsories; Scott was up next and did the same thing. Then Dan Hayden did an extra giant swing and landed the wrong way, dislocating his ankle. We just couldn't get it together, as a team or, consequently, as individuals. During my high bar routine in the optionals, I fell off the bar. Defeat had become infectious. The USA team did not take the gold at the World Championships. Only one year after the 1984 Olympics, we finished eighth. I felt it was my fault.

At this point I had hired a new manager, Nancy Phillips. Although Nancy was based in New York, she was a godsend in coordinating my schedule of appearances and making sure I was where I needed to be on any given day. God knows *I* didn't know where I was!

Nancy had arranged for me to see another of what I once thought was a dream come true. She had been working with a car dealer to get me a very special car to use for a full year, and she was going to deliver it to me in Montreal right after the Championships. It was going to be my baby—it was a brand-new gold Corvette. Gold, reminiscent of 1984. *Gold*, symbolizing my success.

She drove the Corvette to Montreal with my mom, and when I saw the car, I almost cried. I was so angry with myself for my lousy performance. I knew I didn't deserve it.

"Take it back," I wanted to say. But the deal had been done. Once I had equated the fantasy of driving a Corvette with success; now, whenever I looked at that car, I thought of my defeat. I had not succeeded; I was not entitled to the reward. And the color made it even worse. Was I now going to have to *buy* my gold? I ached with self-disgust.

Nancy flew back to New York, and Mom and I drove back to West Springfield, each mile adding to the anger at my performance. Here I was, twenty-three years old, driving a car I never in my wildest dreams thought I would be able to afford, and I was depressed. That's when I realized how insignificant material things are if you don't feel good about yourself first.

When I competed, and even when I worked out, I always had an immense sense of gratification when I had done a good job. Driving my dream car could not come close to that satisfaction; I simply had not earned the privilege.

I went back to L.A., then returned home for Christmas. I spent my vacation training at the University of Massachusetts, Springfield College and Southern Connecticut State University. It seemed that every time I went to a gym someone would come up to me and say,

"Gee, too bad about the World Championships." Then they would look at my car and add, "Nice car!"

Each moment became another sting, another reinforcement of the disappointment I felt in myself.

Not long ago I saw a sign along the roadside which read: "The things which matter most in life aren't things." I was quickly reminded of the Corvette, and grimly aware of its significance.

13

stopped all appearances. I said no to every speaking opportunity and exhibition. If I was ever going to be happy with myself again, I was going to go back to my commitment.

The next important meet was the USA Championships in June 1986. When I returned to Los Angeles just after New Year's, it was all business.

"I'm going to win this one, dammit," I promised myself every day, a hundred times.

I threw myself back into training and concentrated on working out and on completing school. By the time the Championships arrived, I had finished my last paper in my hotel room, just before warm-ups, securing my degree in psychology. Then I went out and did the best I could.

After the first event, I never relinquished my lead. On the second day of competition, while warming up, I reached up in under the pommel horse to adjust the pommels and dislocated my thumb. It didn't matter; nothing mattered. I was going to win; there was no way I wasn't.

I blasted through the optionals without hesitation, confident in my determination and totally focused on the thought that I deserved to win.

It was an easy victory. Like Peter, Mitch, Bart and Jim Hartung before me, I was now the Champion of the USA. It seemed as though I was back on track.

It was no mystery to me why I had won the Championships: I was simply better prepared, both physically and emotionally. I had shifted all the distractions from my life, and had refound my dream. Yes, there were sacrifices. At times maybe I could have done one speech or one exhibition with little or no interruption to my workout schedule, but I didn't. By giving up the monetary rewards it was as though I had put one more chip in my corner—given myself one more edge toward victory. And when I said to myself, "You can do it, Tim. You're going to win this one," I had only to count up those chips and then I was able to believe what I was saying.

There was a month between the Championships and the next important competition, the Goodwill Games. This was the first year of the games, which were developed to provide this type of competition every year: there is always a World Championship meet during the year before and the year after the Olympic Games; the Goodwill Games were to be held the year in between.

I had the opportunity to go to a gymnastics camp and make some money for appearances and coaching while I was training. I still needed money. In order to maintain my amateur status, a chunk of all my earnings were retained by the USGF. The rest was kept in a trust fund for me: after my agent, manager and attorneys were paid, I was only allowed to withdraw a restricted amount each month. To keep the "cash flow" fluid, it made sense to take this job. It had been such a long time since I'd worked, and it didn't seem like it could possibly affect my performance at the Goodwill Games.

But at that level, a month is a long time for an athlete to be away from his regular routine, his regular gym. When you're trying to compete with the best in the world you've got to be ready. Even though

I was the top gymnast in the country—no, *especially* because I was the top gymnast in the country—breaking my routine could be devastating. But I thought I had it licked. Trying to train at the camp, however, proved next to impossible. I'd be on the high bar practicing those difficult release skills and suddenly from out of nowhere appeared a few little kids.

"Can we have your autograph, Tim?" they'd call up to me.

I'd be practicing a tumbling routine on the floor and would flip to the edge of the mat to be greeted by small, smiling faces.

"Can you show us how to do that, Tim?"

There was no way my concentration was in focus.

The games were held in Moscow, and it was a great thrill for me that, because I was the top qualifier, Abie Grossfeld selected Yefim as a coaching assistant. When Yefim had emigrated from Russia he had left many family members and friends behind, and through my success I was now able to give him the small gift of a visit to his homeland— small in relation to the dedication and hard work he had given me.

But obstacles loomed.

When Yefim had applied to leave the Soviet Union in 1979, the human rights of the Russian people were not as exercisable as they are today. He had to quit his job, declare that he was against the Soviet system, and, in essence, prepare never to return again. In the United States, he applied for American citizenship, but the process was lengthy. Now, seven years later, he had the opportunity to visit "home," but without that citizenship he couldn't get the proper visa. It took a lot of cutting through red tape, but finally, just before we were to leave, his citizenship—and visa—came through. But Yefim still had to make it past immigration in Moscow.

Sitting on the plane I looked over at Yefim and was reminded of my experience in East Germany so many years before. Would he be greeted by angry guards? Would he be interrogated, intimidated, held a virtual prisoner?

When we landed, I knew one thing to expect: we were told to line up, single file, and present our passports individually to the grim-faced official in the glass booth.

I went through first, then waited what seemed like an eternity. The cold, concrete walls inside the terminal were threatening. The statuelike stares of the gray-uniformed, heavily armed guards made me turn away in fear. I checked my watch. I checked it again. Suddenly, I heard a familiar voice.

"Timmy!" It was Yefim, walking toward me, waving his passport. "What are you waiting for? Come on, we've got a meet to win!"

He had made it.

Moscow was as I'd remembered it from the 1981 World Championships, with one exception: it was uncharacteristically cold for July. As the starkness settled over the city at night, I should have seen it as an omen. In addition to the cold, this was right after the Chernobyl disaster and people were skittish.

"Under no circumstances is anyone to eat dairy products," was the warning we received.

Before the games began I was able to meet some of Yefim's family and old friends. They were from Kiev, precariously close to where the nuclear disaster had occurred. It was a wonderful feeling when I saw Yefim with them; I knew he had long ago given up hope of seeing any of them again, and that he had been especially concerned when the news of Chernobyl reached the States. Though Yefim is now a competitor against old teammates and completely committed to the United States, he still deeply feels his ties to the Russian people. They are his people; they are his heritage. Witnessing the bond shared between them, I admired the sacrifice Yefim had made to come to our country, and I wondered if I would have been strong enough to do the same.

For once, communicating in the Soviet Union was easy—Yefim was a superb translator, which was essential when trying to convey "gymnastics talk" to everyone at the meet. With him along, it was suddenly much easier to talk with so many gymnasts I had long respected, including Soviet Union greats Vladimir Artemov and Dmitri Bilozerchev.

Vladimir is dark blond with a lean, sleek build that makes him look like he could indeed "fly through the air with the greatest of ease." (He went on to become the star of the 1988 Olympics in Seoul, capturing the gold All-Around, high bar and parallel bars with a silver on floor.) It was kind of spooky because his teammate, Dmitri, was dark and powerful-looking—together they resembled the physical differences between Peter and myself.

But Dmitri wasn't competing in the Goodwill Games: he was trying to come back from a horrible car accident in 1985 that had shattered the bones in his leg in forty places and had nearly resulted in amputation. I watched him walk down the stairs of the arena, obviously trying not to limp, trying to maintain the confident stance indicative of a Soviet gymnast. (Next to them, I always felt we looked like dropouts from a course on proper posture.) But Dmitri's pain was there, etched in the tension on his face. I could not imagine the courage it must have taken to come back from such an injury.

My struggle at the games was a different one. Physically, I thought I was in great shape; mentally, I thought I was prepared. I was not. My month's hiatus from rigorous training was about to leave its devastating mark and result in the worst performance of my career.

Here I was—the Champion of the USA—and I screwed up on everything. I stank on rings. I touched the floor after the vault. And, God, when I was finally doing a decent routine on the pommel horse my hand missed the end of the horse and I did a front flip, landing on my back. I had never done that before. I was ready to quit. My brother-in-law's words stung in my mind: *You just don't look like the same gymnast out there.* How could I have been such a champion only the month before and now look like a high school kid at his first regional meet? This made my disastrous performance at the 1985 World Championships look like gold medal material.

Then, as if my performance wasn't humiliating enough, I did something really stupid. Right after the competition I was surrounded by reporters.

"What happened to you out there?"

"Are you considering retiring now?"

"As our top U.S. gymnast, why do you think you did so poorly?"

The media fired questions at me, increasing my anger with myself. For the first time, I totally lost my cool.

"It's not my fault!" I bellowed like a child. "Our system doesn't work!"

"Explain that, please."

"Almost every other country in the world pays their top amateur athletes at least a living wage. Our country wants to have athletes to be proud of, but they're not willing to help."

"Could you be more specific?"

"Sure! In order to support myself, I had to break training. You can't get more specific than that."

Man, did I sound like a crybaby. But worst of all, I had broken a cardinal rule—you never make excuses to the press. Even though I felt very deeply about what I said, in my anger the criticism came across much stronger than I would have wanted. I loved gymnastics, and, for the most part, gymnastics had treated me well. But now I had been badly defeated and I was making a fool of myself.

Vladimir saw the frustration on my face. He walked over to me after the reporters scurried off and spoke to me in clear, unbroken English.

"Tim, we are not machines," he said.

I have recalled those words often, and silently thanked him for vocalizing this reality.

The next day my story ran in newspapers all over the country. Reading my words in print was even worse than saying them in the heat of my anger, and I hastily tried to apologize to the USGF. They were not pleased, and I don't blame them.

When I remember this embarrassment today, my only consolation is that now our top gymnasts do receive a stipend for living and training expenses. Maybe my untimely blowup provided the catalyst to alter those rules. I'll never know. As distressed as I still feel about my angry words, I am at least pleased that other gymnasts will not have to go through what I did.

I was also so angry with my lousy performance that I stopped eating. Stupid, I know, but I couldn't eat for two days. It was as if I was punishing myself for, once again, letting my team down, letting myself down.

Right after the games we were scheduled for a meet in West Germany. But first, we had to get Yefim out of the Soviet Union.

Walking through customs I was at once conscious of something I'd never before seen in Yefim: he was scared. Getting him into the country had gone pretty smoothly, but, I suddenly thought, what if they wouldn't let him leave? His usually cheerful face was masked with fear, and I sensed he was thinking the same thing.

We reached the line. This time, Yefim was in front of me. I watched as he walked to the smoky window, his slight frame moving tentatively, one hand nervously smoothing his short black hair. He slid his passport through the opening in the glass. I shifted my weight from one foot to the other, steadily watching from the regulation distance. Waiting. Once again, waiting.

The man behind the window scrutinized the passport, scrutinized Yefim. Finally, he stamped the passport. Yefim quickly retrieved it, then turned to pass through the gate. I moved forward to the window, never taking my eyes off Yefim's back. I envisioned one of the guards grabbing him and thrusting a machine gun into his side. It didn't happen.

It wasn't until we were on the plane and safely taxiing down the runaway that I spoke to him.

"Yefim, you looked a little bit scared back there," I said.

"Scared? Me?" he asked. "No, I was fine!" Then he smiled a strange little smile and I knew just how scared he had been. Damn scared.

We landed in West Germany and I began to feel the tension ease. It is such a beautiful place, with breathtaking scenery and fans who simply go nuts over gymnastics. After my depression following the Goodwill Games, I was determined not to let that happen again. I managed to control my attitude and give the meet my old, determined self. Somehow, I won the competition. Guess I'd had it in me all along.

It had been a long summer with many competitions and much stress. As a perk to its athletes, the USGF arranged for us to take a sort of holiday after the West German meet, by spending a week (and doing an exhibition!) on the magnificent island of Sardinia, west of the southern Italian coast. There was no doubt that I needed a vacation. I was physically exhausted, and mentally spent. I needed to renew my spirit, and needed it badly. Between that terrible performance at the Goodwill Games and that temper-tantrum interview, yes, I needed a vacation. But I knew my own mind, and I knew what I had to do.

"I'm not going," I announced to Yefim.

"What? Are you crazy?"

"I'm not going," I repeated. I didn't deserve a vacation then, any more than I had deserved the Corvette after the 1985 Championships. I knew I wouldn't have enjoyed it; I knew all I would be thinking of was my disastrous performance. Right then I just didn't like myself very much. The only way for me to get it out of my system was to work out my frustrations in the gym, and, once and for all, to face my future head-on. The team flew to Sardinia; I went back to Los Angeles.

I had to decide what I really wanted. Did I want money? Did I want to hang on to the celebrity status? Or did I want to be a gymnast? "Well, come on, Tim," I told myself, "by now you know the answer to that."

When Yefim returned to L.A., I sat down with him.

"I want to go on to 1988, Yefim," I said. "I want to go to Seoul."

"Well, then, we have two years, don't we?" he replied. "Two years of hard work ahead of us. Are you going to give up show business?"

I thought for a moment, knowing that he would—as would I—certainly hold me to the next words I said. "If that's what it takes," I finally answered.

But giving up the money-making opportunities was only the first of the decisions: Yefim then insisted I have surgery done on both ankles to remove the bone chips that had accumulated over so many years of slamming my body into the floor.

"If you're going to Seoul you're going to have to land perfectly. And you can't land perfectly on those," he said, pointing to my bumpy, tired-out ankles.

The operations were performed: "invasive" surgery on my left ankle, orthoscopic surgery on my right. I was back on crutches again, and moved into Yefim's house while I recuperated.

It was great to be back in a family environment. Yefim's wife, Nina, couldn't do enough for me, and their sixteen-year-old daughter, Julia, made me feel like I had a kid sister around once again. But the Furman household was a totally new experience for me: this was not your typical American home where the television blared as hamburgers fried on the stove, for they had brought to this country their rich Soviet culture, and it was an honor to be a part of it.

Every evening they took a walk, then returned home to read or work. The house was small and neat, filled with antique furniture of superb craftsmanship and appointed with tasteful paintings and treasures befitting their centuries-old heritage. I learned to love borscht, and, as the Italians are known for enjoying their wine, so the Russians are for their vodka. I had my first shot of vodka there: I decided I much preferred the borscht.

Every day while at Yefim's I worked on my psyche. If I started focusing on the '88 Olympics now, I would be that much ahead of the game when I was able to return to the gym. It worked. I was off crutches in no time, back to my apartment and back into training.

"This time it's going to be different," I kept reassuring Yefim. "No more fooling around, no more excuses."

Age was creeping up on me: I was now twenty-four. The Games in 1988 would be my last chance, and I was going to go out a winner.

PART III

THE
NIGHTMARE

14

E very so often I'd hear from one of the guys: Peter called from Aspen, where he was giving a motivational speech, and he and Donna were enjoying the skiing; Bart Conner and Jim Hartung called from aboard a cruise ship where they were doing an exhibition; Mitch called from location where he was making a movie. They were all making money, having a great time and continuing to reap the rewards of the gold.

What the hell was I doing in a gym? It did not make my workouts any easier, but I think it helped to reinforce my commitment. If I was making this sacrifice, I was going to make it all the way.

Once I announced that I was going to try for the 1988 Olympics, the critics came out once again. While there was enthusiasm from the media, other "people" in the gymnastics circuit began talking.

"Is he just going for the publicity?"

"He's had his glory, now he wants more."

"When is this kid going to quit?"

Those negative whispers really hurt me. To begin with, if the people saying them knew anything about me, knew me at all, they would have known better. I wanted no more glory; I wanted gymnastics. Gymnastics poured through every bone and muscle in my body. I wasn't ready to quit.

Now that my ankles were stronger than they'd been in years, I began preparing for the 1987 McDonald's American Cup to be held in March. I had rebuilt my strength and felt I was in better physical shape than I'd been either at the Olympics or the 1986 Championships. There would be no more humiliation such as that at the Goodwill Games: that was all behind me now. I knew that.

Some dates stick in your mind forever. For me, July 31, 1984, was one date I'd never forget. And then there was February 17, 1987.

I was working out on the high bar, my last routine of the day. It was Friday, the last day of the week's training. I was in the gym at the John Wooden Center, and Mark Caso was there. He had retired from gymnastics, but came by the gym once in a while for a workout. I was practicing that difficult release skill—the "Gienger." I had done it thousands of times. I had missed the bar plenty of times before, but I had also caught it plenty of times.

This time, I sensed I would catch it, no problem.

In that split second when you must decide whether you're going to catch the bar or you're going to fall, you must prepare yourself for the next stage. If you think you're going to miss it, you have to get ready to fall.

"I can catch it for sure," I thought as I flew through the air. I felt on target. My timing was fine.

I missed the bar. I came down wrong. I landed directly on my head.

I heard a loud crack. A bolt of pain flashed through my body like an electric shock. Oh my god, I thought. But then, with the true athlete's nondestructive mentality, my next reaction was typical. "It's okay, I'm fine."

Mark was across the gym and heard the crack. He came running over to the high bar and stood over me, his face ashen. This was the way he had broken his neck so many years before.

"Tim!" he screamed. It was all he could say.

I lay there a few seconds, then knew what I had to do: I had to try and move my legs, then my arms. Was I paralyzed? They moved. I had to turn my head. Slowly, through the pain, I tried to turn it a little. It moved. God, it moved. I was going to be all right.

I didn't see a doctor right away, but after a couple of days, when the pain grew worse, Mark convinced me to go. I went into the training room, where a doctor is always present. Unfortunately, the "internal athlete" took over.

"How bad is the pain?" the doctor asked.

"Not bad. The muscles are just sore." Any nonathlete would have been screaming with the pain. But something happens to us. It's as though we think we're indestructible. And when it comes to our sport, we often temper an injury or illness because our greatest fear is being told we can't compete. It made no sense that I was minimizing the problem, but I was following in the path of other gymnasts before me—great gymnasts like Fujimoto of Japan who, during the 1976 Olympics, clinched the gold medal for his team with his outstanding performance on rings, which included a magnificent dismount that he stuck cold . . . on a broken leg. The team had needed his score to capture the gold. He was not about to let a little thing like a broken leg stop him.

The soreness of my neck now could not possibly compare with the pain Fujimoto must have felt. And the McDonald's American Cup was just a few weeks away.

"I'm okay, really," I said to the doctor. "I'm going to be fine." He dismissed me, feeling that no tests were necessary.

About a week and a half later I went to Sacramento to do an exhibition at the Carnelian Festival. Although I had given up the hectic schedule of appearances, I was using this as a dress rehearsal for the American Cup. Peter was doing the exhibition, too, and he met me at the airport.

"How's it going?" he asked.

"Well, you're not going to believe this, but I missed a Gienger. Landed on my head."

We climbed in the van that would take us to the festival.

"It really hurts, but it's not broken."

I knew Peter would understand the magnitude of what I had done: Mark had been his roommate when Mark broke his neck, and Peter was one of the ones who spent so many months helping him rehabilitate.

"You're lucky, man, you know that?"

"Yeah," I said, unconsciously rubbing my neck.

During warm-ups for the exhibition I was going through my floor routine. Things were going pretty well. Then I pressed to a handstand and, suddenly, my left arm buckled. Peter noticed.

"What happened? That was really weird," he said.

I answered as best I could. "I've no idea. I can't use my left arm. It's not working."

I went to the parallel bars and did a simple straddle "L" press to a handstand. I tried to press out of it, and the same thing happened. My arm completely buckled.

"Man, what's wrong?" Peter sounded concerned. "Nobody on the planet does a press from a straddle 'L' like you do!"

But I simply had no strength in my left arm. It was lifeless. And now I couldn't even perform what had been one of the easiest skills for me. A skill I had been doing, and doing well, since I was eleven years old.

"When you get back to L.A. you'd better get yourself to a doctor right away, no fooling around," he said.

Peter was right. Something was very wrong.

I did a lousy job at the exhibition, though the enthusiastic crowd hardly seemed to notice when I could barely get myself above the rings. After we were finished, I reached down to pick up my gym bag. It felt heavy, as though it was filled with bowling balls instead of lightweight, chalky ring grips.

Back at UCLA things weren't improving. I tried to do a chin-up—I couldn't. My entire left side was not working. I couldn't even lift my arm over my head. I went to the doctor.

This time, I didn't say, "I'm okay, I'm fine." Instead I said, "I think something's wrong. Really wrong. You'd better check me out."

The doctor in the athletic training room that evening was Bert Mandelbaum, an orthopedic surgeon. I had seen him around a few times, but had never been treated by him for anything. I will always be grateful that he was the one there when I finally went to get checked out. He examined me, studying the strength deficit, listening carefully when I described the pain.

"I think we should do an MRI," he said, without hesitation.

"I just need to know if I can go to the American Cup," I said.

An ordinary doctor might have discouraged me immediately, but Dr. Mandelbaum was used to working with athletes—he knows we're a little bit nuts. He arranged for the test and told me to go home when it was finished. He would call me there later.

I have never been prone to claustrophobia, but the MRI scan would change that. Lying in a coffinlike tube, immobilized by the straps across my body, my nervous energy began to take over. It was dark in the tunnel, and there were frightening sounds—*clink, clink, clunk.* Pause. *Clink, clink, clunk.* I kept thinking things were gong to fall on me, crush me, suffocate me. It was as though I was trapped in the middle of a "Star Wars" movie. I tried to focus on telling myself that I was going to be okay, but deep inside I knew that wasn't true.

After what seemed like an eternity, the test was over. I asked the technician what she thought, how did it look to her?

She replied somberly, "Well, I really can't tell."

I didn't believe her for a minute.

Back at my apartment I was resting on the couch when the phone rang. It was Dr. Mandelbaum.

"Tim, the results are back," he said. His voice was not cheerful.

A cold chill engulfed my body.

"I'm going to be up front with you," he continued. "It's not good. You have a ruptured disc with a tremendous number of complications.

It looks like you'll probably have to have surgery. I don't think at this point you should be thinking about the American Cup."

I felt weak all over. I began to shake.

In my mind, his words seemed to say, "You'll never be able to compete again." I felt sick.

"I'd like to see you tonight in the training room," he added.

I hung up the phone. I was alone in my apartment, sitting directly across from the couch. I looked across at the wall behind the couch, at the poster-size photograph of the opening ceremonies of the 1984 Olympics. I looked down at the floor, and I cried. This was the first time I had cried over gymnastics, over the sport I had loved most of my life, over the very root of my existence. How could gymnastics do this to me? No one had yet vocalized it, but I felt certain that people expected me never to compete again.

Later that evening I met with Dr. Mandelbaum. He immediately put a cervical collar around my neck.

"I've been doing some thinking," he said. "I've also conferred with some other doctors, all of whom feel surgery is necessary. But I think we may have another option. Surgery would mean fusing the bone together. It is risky, and chances are it would end your career."

Chances are it would end your career. I was numb.

He showed me the test results, pointing out the problem. He then told me he had arranged for us to go together to see a neck specialist the following day, where they would discuss my options.

Thankfully, my roommate at the time, Luc Tuerlings, was in the training room, and he drove me home. I remember thinking in the car how amazing it is that I could have such a major problem and still be walking around. My mind kept telling me over and over: This is really happening. This is really serious. But it was hard to comprehend.

The neck specialist agreed with Dr. Mandelbaum's diagnosis. Then they told me about the treatment "option"—cervical traction in the hospital for an indefinite amount of time, depending on how I responded. But they were both emphatic in saying this might not work. Even if it did, the ruptured disc would always be there, possibly requiring surgery down the road. Going into traction was, at best, a long shot.

I opted for the traction. The last thing I wanted was to have surgery on my neck. Dr. Mandelbaum also explained that the nerve damage had taken such a long time to show up because it's often like autumn leaves on a tree. As they die, they slowly fall off, withering until they are no longer there. Unlike an injury which you can feel on impact, nerve damage can be a sneaky, slow-to-surface problem.

I called home and told my mom I was going into the hospital. She kept pumping me for information, but I remained vague and upbeat.

"It's just a few days of traction. I'll be as good as new."

She wanted to come to L.A.

"There's no need, Mom," I said. "Please don't. I'll be fine." I sounded more convincing than I felt.

One of the first things Dr. Mandelbaum did before I was set up in traction was ask a very important question.

"What about the press? Do you want to see them?"

"No. Absolutely not."

Because I was going to be in the hospital throughout the American Cup competition, CBS had already requested to do a live remote from my bedside. I couldn't have handled that.

In the hospital, they had me lie flat on my back and affixed under my chin an appliance that ran up the back of my head. They held this down with weights. If I'd thought I'd had claustrophobia during the MRI test, that was nothing compared with this. To help the pain and to calm my nerves, they put me on medication.

"Don't be frightened if you start hallucinating or thinking strange, confused thoughts," the doctor warned.

Great. Just what I needed. To be totally immobile and not be able to use the one thing that had always saved my sanity—my mind. I stared at the ceiling and tried to build up my resolve. This was going to be "home" for the next who-knew-how-many days. I lay there, paralyzed by weights and anchors. I slipped into a dark depression.

Many of my friends came by to see me. I was grateful for their support, but I really didn't want to see anyone. I didn't want to see their faces, to read their unspoken words. I couldn't do a thing. Watching television was next to impossible because of the angle of the set. Besides, I didn't have the heart to see the American Cup. I couldn't read, either. They gave me some prism glasses which are supposed to make it easy to read a book while you're lying down, but the disjointed image through the lenses made me sick to my stomach.

As each day passed, the nausea from the medication increased. Someone had brought my favorite, Mrs. Fields chocolate chip cookies. They sat, growing stale, on the nightstand. And the worst came each day—three times a day—when I heard the rattle of the carts carrying the meal trays down the halls. The association I made between that sound and food made me instantly sick: it is a sensation that has followed me to this day.

The cards and letters seemed to be in even greater quantity than those I received after the gold. I could not read them; but often a nurse or a visiting friend would read them for me, trying to pick up my spirits. It didn't work.

Once the phone rang, and I was in no mood to answer it. I didn't want to talk to anyone, especially not the press, especially not my mother. I was afraid she would know by the sound of my voice how bad I was. I lay there staring at the ceiling, willing the phone to stop ringing. It didn't. Whoever it was wasn't going to quit. Finally I struggled to reach it.

"Hey, man, how goes it?" came the chipper voice of Jim Hartung on the other end of the line.

I was relieved it was him.

"God, Jim, didn't you get the hint? I'm lousy and I don't want to talk to anyone!" At least with Jim I could be honest. But he rambled on for a few minutes, undaunted by my reaction. After we hung up, I had to admit I felt better. There was nothing like an '84 teammate to perk up my spirits. Now I make it a point to call other gymnasts if I hear they've been hospitalized.

After nine days Dr. Mandelbaum told me it was time for another MRI. "Let's see how we're doing," he said.

The relief of being removed from traction was minimized by what was ahead: another long session locked in a tube; an act that would determine my destiny. I was feeling so sorry for myself at this point that I was overreacting to everything.

The orderly arrived and helped me onto a gurney, stabilizing my head so my gaze was directed straight at the ceiling. He talked too much.

"You'll be out of here in no time," he chattered, maneuvering the gurney down the hall. "Yup, in no time. Just you wait and see."

What did he care? He didn't know me.

"Yup, everything's going to turn out okay."

This must be the standard line used by all orderlies. Why didn't he just shut up?

From the corner of one eye I saw heads whizzing past me, hands gripping raised bed rails, obviously rushing an emergency victim somewhere. Hard rubber wheels rattled from the speed; the faces of the nurses and doctors were frozen.

We made it to the elevator and the doors swished open, revealing another gurney, this one decked with tube after tube suspended from plastic IV bags, trailing, I knew, into the veins of some pain-racked soul. One bag was red, thick with blood.

My orderly stepped aside, allowing the other one to move his gurney from the elevator. As the bed slid by mine, I heard a low moan come from the patient. I was glad I could only look up; I didn't want to see what the person might look like. *It must be someone old*, I rationalized.

The other gurney disappeared; the orderly pushed mine over the doorway into the elevator. Oh. The bump. The pain. The doors closed and I sensed we were going down . . . down to the darkness of the huge hospital. Whatever happened next would determine my future.

This time, it wasn't the test that was scary. This time, as I lay in the now familiar tube, listening to the mechanical sounds grinding out my destiny, I was filled with fear about the results.

Back in my room the clock ticked slowly. I tried to accept the fact that my career was over, that gymnastics would no longer be part of my life. I reviewed the years as snapshots in my mind: winning the Western Massachusetts Championships; my first attempt to make the Junior National team; my first trip to UCLA; making the Olympic team; wining the Gold. Pain has a way of blocking out the bad things—the 1985 Championships, the 1986 Goodwill Games. If I was going to have to give up my career, I had to admit it had been a wonderful one. I would not have traded it for anything in the world.

Dr. Mandelbaum arrived at my door. He was smiling.

"It looks good," he said.

Tears sprang to my eyes. It wasn't over after all. Suddenly my mind clicked from "My god, my life is over" to "My god, I've got to get out of here. There are only eight more months to the World Championships. I've got to get ready. I've got to get to work."

But Dr. Mandelbaum wasn't about to let me off that easy.

"I'd like you here another day, Tim," he said. "Another day will help even more."

That last day in the hospital seemed ten times longer than the days before.

I left the hospital wearing a huge cervical collar which was to be part of me for the next three months. I was still in pain, but comforted by the thought that I hadn't needed surgery. Not yet, anyway.

My roommate, Luc, the Belgian National Champion who was training at UCLA, was a great help to me—it's amazing how little you can do for yourself when you're trapped in one of those collars! Washing dishes was risky—I couldn't bend my head down far enough to see if I was getting them clean. Doing my laundry was impossible, as were so many other things I had always taken for granted . . . like walking around campus checking out the girls. It was really frustrating that I was unable to do "double takes" when a great-looking girl walked by.

I went back to the gym with determination. In order to get there I had to drive my car, and it's pretty scary to be on the San Diego

Freeway when you can't turn your head. More than once when I had to change lanes I closed my eyes, put on my blinker and prayed. I certainly wouldn't recommend this to anyone.

Beyond my neck itself, an even bigger hurdle I had to overcome was the nerve damage. My body was now about 25 percent weaker on the left side, and gymnastics demands great strength of the upper body. It would not have been unlike a boxer losing one-quarter of his punching power or a runner losing one-quarter of his speed. I figured out what I had to do: I simply would have to work 25 percent harder than ever before. My natural ability had been decreased, but if I worked harder, I could compensate. The Bull was going to make it back.

Performing even the standard rigorous strength-conditioning exercises wasn't doing the trick, because as I was increasing the strength on my left side, that on my right side was increasing, too. I had to get the strength to become *equal* once again, and this would never work. I began doing strength exercises on my left side only.

Dr. Mandelbaum watched my progress steadily. He introduced me to a physical therapist named James Zackezewski, and had us set up a schedule of rehabilitation. "Zack" and I got along great right from the start, especially after he told me his hometown was Easthampton, Massachusetts—a town a stone's throw from West Springfield. It was almost like having family there!

As he worked with me day after day my depression lifted. The pain of therapy was something I came to welcome, because each day meant I was one step closer to healing. Zack also was great about working on my other injuries, too.

"Just because your neck is what's bothering you most now, doesn't mean we should ignore other problems," he said.

Other problems? Oh, yeah. My ankles, which were sore from time to time, and my wrists, which still bothered me a little. Somehow I'd forgotten about those things, they seemed so minor. And they *were* minor. But Zack's thorough treatment of me as a total being helped improve those other weaknesses considerably.

When I finally was able to work out on the apparatus again, it was hell. The collar was so restrictive it impaired my vision on the pommel horse. Though you never actually look directly at the pommels, you see them from your peripheral vision, and you know where your hands should go next. Now I couldn't see them at all, and, with my head fixed perfectly straight, I had to rely on my years of familiarity to know where they were.

Oddly, wearing the brace was beneficial for one skill on the parallel bars: the "peach basket." As you drop below the bars, then come back up into a handstand, a common mistake is to lift your head too soon. But because I had no control over what my head could do, I couldn't lift it too soon, and I was therefore able to do a perfect peach basket! It was kind of like one small silver lining in that big black cloud that hung over me.

But by far the worst part was doing skills that were totally dependent on equal strength on both sides. For a long time, whenever I tried the vault I ran down the runway and hit the vault harder with my right side than my left, causing me to twist in the air and land lopsided. It was the same with the floor exercise: I would do a perfect tumbling sequence, then, upon landing, end up off-center on the mat.

The rings were the worst. Each time I tried to swing up to a handstand, my body twisted. When I tried to dismount, I pushed the rings in front of me, which you need to do to get them out of the way: my right ring would push out fine, but my left one didn't go as far and would come back to slap me on the side.

With each routine I kept yelling in my mind to my left side, "Push! Push!" but the message wasn't reaching the muscles it needed to. It was frustrating, because it went against my character. It seemed that no matter how hard I worked I just had no control over this thing. Not yet, anyway. But I would.

What made it worse was that I knew the strength was there. The muscles could work if I could just get the message to them! It was so frustrating.

There was yet another obstacle I had to face, though I tried not to think about it. I had to, sometime soon, try another Gienger on the high bar. After so many months of watching Mark Caso trying to conquer his fear of gymnastics after he had broken his neck, I knew this was going to be the hardest thing of all: I could never take another fall like that again without serious consequences. I also knew the sooner I could get it over with, the better.

I had been doing some basic skills on the bar—simple turns, giant swings, anything that wasn't risky. One day I was working out on the bar, and after one turn a little voice inside my head said, "Okay, Tim, it's time. Next, you're going to do it. You're going to do the Gienger."

Without thinking about it further, I mounted the bar again and just let my body take over, hoping it would remember what to do. It was doing fine; I was surprisingly relaxed. I let go of the bar, turned, then . . . my god, it was there. I caught the bar. I had done the Gienger. Everything was going to be all right. Everything was going to be fine.

15

In the spring I was asked to appear on "Good Morning, America." It was cumbersome to travel with the neck brace still on, but I wanted very badly to do the program. I wanted to show America I was on the comeback trail. On the plane I sat next to the actor Steve Guttenberg. Steve was on his way back to New York after the Academy Awards, as were many of the other passengers. One of them was on his way to deliver an Oscar to a friend. The statue was passed around, and I got to hold it for a few seconds.

"Oh, yeah," I thought. "Gold. I remember now. This is what stardom is like." Nineteen eighty-four seemed a lifetime ago.

When I arrived at the studio I was told that Kathleen Sullivan would be doing the interview. As I sat in the waiting room, I thought about the last time I had seen Kathleen—when she interviewed us right after we'd won the gold, when my success was at its peak. Now I would be facing her with a whole different story to tell. I suddenly felt broken, beaten. Could I ever again be that same athlete of the 1984 Games? Could I ever hope to achieve my goals? I touched the edge of the neck brace. Depression crept in.

"Okay, Tim, you're next." A producer beckoned. I walked onto the set and saw Kathleen. My depression deepened.

I had not anticipated that my reaction would be so strong: I also had not anticipated another thing—my mother was watching the show.

"What is that thing around your neck, Timothy?" she cried into the phone right after the broadcast. "You're hurt very badly, aren't you? Why didn't you tell me?"

"I didn't tell you because I didn't want to upset you, Mom," I said. "There was nothing you could do. But I'm okay now, really I am. The brace is almost ready to come off."

It must have been quite a shock for her to see me like that, and I know now that not telling her beforehand was a mistake. But at the time I wasn't thinking clearly; I guess I just didn't want to admit to myself how bad the injury was.

Back in L.A. the guys were great about stopping by the gym to check up on me. Mark and his brother, Chris, Mitch and Robbie Campbell all came one day and decided we should go for pizza after workout. Long before '84 we had found a great place in Westwood—Santo Pietro—a classy Italian restaurant, with the best pizza in the West. The owner of the restaurant had always been good to us and insisted on giving us free food during the hard times, before we were "anyone."

It was a chilly night, and we left the gym, our mouths watering for Santo Pietro's pizza. I was bundled in a huge sweater covering the enormous brace, making me look like an alien being.

As we sank our teeth into the steamy mozzarella, Mark talked to me about his neck, and about some of the things that helped him in his rehabilitation. We had all been part of Mark's rehabilitation: now it was my turn to be the recipient of advice—some of which was the same advice I'd given Mark.

Just as the mood was getting somber, Mitch spoke up.

"Personally, I think it stinks. I mean, I never had an injury good enough to get me on 'Good Morning, America'! I had to earn my publicity!"

"Come to think of it, I never did, either!" chimed in Chris.

"Seems to me like it's been a ploy all along to get some attention," Mitch continued. "What better way to get sympathy than to go on national television with this huge concoction strapped to your neck?" Then Mitch did a superb imitation of how stupid I must have looked.

This was a tough group. And they were the best medicine I could have gotten.

It was finally time for the collar to come off. I didn't need Dr. Mandelbaum to tell me twice. I raced into the athletic training room, determined to burn it. I never wanted to see that ugly thing again; I wanted no reminders of what had happened.

Unfortunately, locating a pack of matches in a training room is difficult. I searched and searched, then finally found a crumpled pack with two bent cardboard sticks left. I ripped off the collar and set it in an empty trash barrel. I struck one match and leaned into the barrel, carefully igniting the soft plastic. About a half-inch area turned a bit black, then the match went out. Exasperated, I tried again. This time the collar smoldered somewhat, singeing only about a two-inch area. It gave off a terrible odor, and only charred one side before that match, too, went out. So much for theatrics. I put the lid on the trash barrel and walked away. In my mind the thing had gone up in flames. At last, I was truly on the comeback trail.

I was able to compete in the USA Championships that June, the trials for the Pan American Games.

God, how I wanted—needed—to make the team. This time it didn't bother me to listen to the talk: "it's not possible"; "no way"; "he can never do it." I had learned to love it when people said it couldn't be done.

All through my rehabilitation I'd received calls from other athletes, trainers and gymnastics people "in-the-know" who wanted to extend their sympathy for my career being over. These were, for the most part, people who were familiar with the type of injury I had. But I refused to understand what they were talking about. I knew what I wanted, and

I knew I could do it. Now my chance had come to prove them wrong, and to prove to myself I was right.

Though my neck was still a bit sore, I put the discomfort behind me. I ended up fourth overall, even winning the gold on the pommel horse. I left a lot of people openmouthed, and left myself with an enormous amount of satisfaction for a job well done.

Scott Johnson won the meet, and that was great, because it meant that now each of the six members of the 1984 Olympic team had, at one point, become the best gymnast in the USA.

The Pan Am Games were held in Indianapolis that August. As always, we went a few days before the meet to get used to the equipment and become familiar with the arena. After a couple of days, I felt as though I was coming down with the flu.

"Great," I said to my roommate, Scott Johnson. "This is just what I need."

I didn't go to the opening ceremonies, opting instead to sleep. I slept for twenty-four hours straight. The next day Scott made me get out of bed to go to the cafeteria.

"You've got to eat, or you'll have no strength," he reasoned.

I, however, was beyond reason: I was too tired, and my throat was killing me. But Scott didn't give up easily, and he finally convinced me to go with him. It's about a three-quarter-mile walk to where we had to go to eat, and I knew I couldn't make it. Partway there, my legs buckled.

Thinking quickly, Scott flagged down a security cart and had us driven to the cafeteria. Immediately after, I went to see the doctor for the U.S. delegation.

He took a throat culture and did a blood test.

"We'll have the results back in a few days," he told me.

A few days. Hell, the competition would be over by then.

"Come back every time before you eat, and I'll coat your throat with Xylocaine jelly," he said. "It will make the food go down easier."

Not only couldn't I swallow food, I couldn't swallow my own saliva.

So there I was, this incredible, unbelievable, against-all-odds come-back story, practically crawling into the arena, carrying a little paper cup to spit into. For the first time, I seriously considered retiring.

That night the compulsories were held. I was too tired to warm up. When it came time for the meet. I could barely get out of my chair.

We started on the parallel bars, then went to the high bar, floor and pommel horse. Every time I landed after each apparatus, my legs buckled. Not enough for a deduction, but enough to tell me my strength was sapped. Incredibly, I was winning.

Next came the rings. As I tried to power down from a handstand I fell below the rings—a significant deduction. I was shocked. I panicked. What was happening to me now? My emotions were screaming inside me.

Then it was time for the vault—I had no strength there, either. I fell to eighth place in the standings. Man, this comeback stuff was for the birds. I crawled back to the room and slept until just before warm-ups the following day.

During the optionals I was greeted with yet another surprise: during the parallel bars my arms completely buckled twice. It was not a major deduction but it was emotionally distressing. That had never happened before. Something was definitely wrong. I managed to get through the rest of the events and do very well, weak arms, weak legs and all.

There was only one day left of the competition, the finals, and I knew I had to finish. No one but Scott and the doctor knew of my problem. I just didn't want to tell anyone; I was tired of making excuses and I felt as though complaining would make me sound like I was trying to get out of the competition. Which, deep down, I really wanted to do.

I decided then that the critics had been right. As I stuffed my face into my pillow that night, eager for the long-awaited sleep, I faced the fact that perhaps I had, after all, expected too much of myself to come back from the neck injury. I was washed-up; I was history. I drifted off to sleep.

The next morning I awoke feeling better. I was still a little weak, but my throat wasn't as sore and I could tell that some of my strength had returned. Not much, but some. Maybe enough to get through this meet with a respectable finish. Maybe enough not to embarrass myself again.

I went to the doctor for my Xylocaine, then headed off for the cafeteria with Scott, eager to take the cart, not wanting to take away from what strength I had managed to find during the night. I ate a decent meal and got ready for the finals. I wanted them over with; God, I wanted this meet to be done.

Incredibly, I did great. I ended up in third place overall, even winning the gold on the pommel horse. Nevertheless, I was discouraged. I knew a third-place showing was far worse than I should have done. At this rate I would never make the grade at the World Championships in November. Here we had competed against the Canadians, Cubans, Puerto Ricans, Mexicans and South Americans. There I would be up against the best in the world: the Chinese, the Japanese and the Russians. I had no shot: I was too tired to think about returning to L.A. and training hard.

Immediately after the competition the media swarmed around me.

"Are you disappointed with third place?"

Are you kidding? I was just glad to be done. Sometimes the press asked the strangest questions.

"How do you think you'll do at the World Championships?"

Don't ask.

"Are you still considering retiring?"

Whoever said I had considered it in the first place?

But I smiled through the interviews, trying to keep optimistic. The last thing I wanted was for the press to know how I really felt. I had done that once in Moscow and it almost cost me my respectability, if not my career.

When their questions were exhausted, I went into the training room to shower and change. Just then, the doctor came in.

"The results of your blood test are back," he said.

Oh, yeah, the blood test. I'd forgotten about that.

"Did they show anything?" I asked, more out of politeness than curiosity. I knew the only thing wrong with me was that I was over the hill for gymnastics.

"Yes. It seems you have mononucleosis."

I stood there dumbstruck. "What?" I asked.

He repeated the diagnosis, then added, "If we had known before the meet began, we probably wouldn't have let you compete."

I started to laugh. I wanted to kiss the doctor. He had no idea, but with this news he had given me a new lease on life, on my career. My neck was going to be okay, the nerve damage was going to be fine . . . I simply had mono! I was still a champion . . . I was just sick! If my throat still hadn't been sore I'd have screamed with joy so they could have heard me back in West Springfield. I returned to L.A. and slept for a week.

Yefim was in Pennsylvania with the team, training for the World Championships. When I finally was able to join them, he was like a mother hen.

"Okay, Timmy, time for your nap," he'd say after I'd been working out for a short while. He would give me only one turn on each apparatus, then it was off to bed. It was exasperating, but I knew he was right. I did not, under any circumstances, want to get so sick again. I knew the mono hadn't completely gone away; I knew it was lurking somewhere inside me, just waiting for me to overdo it.

On September 29, we flew to West Germany to train for the Championships. Though they were to be held in Rotterdam, Holland, giving ourselves nearly two weeks of training in Europe beforehand helped acclimate our bodies to the time change and our minds to the continental environment.

To prepare for Rotterdam, we had a small meet at the Stuttgart Sports Center. After the event, I saw someone I hadn't seen for a while, but was anxious to talk with again: Eberhard Gienger.

I shook his hand and said, "How nice to see you again. Your release skill almost killed me a few months ago."

He laughed. I got the impression he had heard it before!

Being in West Germany was always exciting, for the people are truly sports fans. Eberhard himself was a huge star—West German sports heroes are the equivalent of our movie stars. There were always many, many fans packed into the arenas, even for the most insignificant meets, and it helped charge us up for the big event to come.

It was Oktoberfest in West Germany, and the night before we left for Rotterdam we decided to enjoy the celebration—sort of a last hurrah before going on to the Championships. Little did I know it would be my last hurrah for many months to come.

Not far from where we were staying an enormous festival was taking place. I have never seen so many people and so much beer! Waitresses squeezed by us in the big hall, toting trays laden with thirty mugs of sloshing foam; we sat on beer-soaked wooden benches, feasting on sauerkraut and knockwurst, taking in all the unfamiliar sights.

After we ate we cruised the grounds—this certainly wasn't like any of the country fairs back home. Instead of agricultural exhibits there was beer; instead of amusements there was beer; instead of games of chance there was beer! Tent after tent held long rows of tables, and in between the aisles oompah bands decked out in colorful lederhosen led joyful groups in song after song. It was quite an experience.

The next day the bus arrived at our hotel to take us to the airport. As we walked out onto the street we were barraged by people.

"Mr. Daggett! Autograph, please!"

"Mr. Daggett, you are a great sportsman!"

We signed countless autographs and enjoyed the enthusiasm of the West Germans. I was reminded of another time when German people hadn't been so receptive to me—when I lost my passport in East Germany. I shuddered.

We boarded the bus and were off to Rotterdam. My neck felt good, my ankles were fine, and I was psyched. This was going to be the performance of a lifetime. I was ready.

16

It was a long bus ride from the airport to our hotel. I had always wanted to go to Holland to see the storybook villages, colorful tulips and quaint windmills I had read about in school. My brief exploration of Amsterdam years before with Jim Mikus had shown me little. But as I watched out the window of the bus, I realized there were no tulips this time of year, only a dullish gray landscape which seemed to be interrupted everywhere by water. It was just as well: I was there to compete, not to look at the scenery.

Sight-seeing was something I was never able to do while I was in a new place. Unlike others who could take a break from working out and enjoy the unfamiliar surroundings, I was too one-dimensional, too intent on the job ahead of me. I never let myself take advantage of the opportunity given me to see life around me. I closed myself into my own small world and lived for gymnastics. For all I knew I could have been in West Springfield, Oshkosh or Moscow—all I needed was a place to sleep, food to eat and a gym. Now, it happened I was in Rotterdam.

The other guys were dropped off at our hotel; I had been asked to do an interview at the local television station. After that was finished, I was brought to the sports complex where the competition would be held. I was glad: this gave me the chance to do what I always liked to do first—get into the arena and check out the equipment.

Rather than stop and register, I quickly started looking for the competition area, oblivious to the voices that called after me: "You must register first! You must register first!"

Winding my way through the back corridors, past storage rooms, locker rooms and offices, I followed the innate sense I have for finding a gym. I stepped through a doorway and there it was. The equipment was in place, everything was ready.

I went onto the podium and tested the floor for bounciness. It has always amazed me that no matter where you are in the world, the floors are different. Some are cushiony, some are hard as a rock. This one was hard as a rock. It was the last thing we liked. But I quickly passed it off with my nonstop optimism: "It'll be fine," I told myself.

I smiled, thinking of Abie. Whenever we went anywhere we complained about the floors. In the last couple of years he had taken to quickly walking over to the floor first and bouncing on it before we had a chance.

"Feels pretty good to me!" he'd announce, as if to ward off our negative reactions. I think he could have bounced on concrete and said the same: it was all for the good of the team.

Next I checked out the floor exercise area to see which corner I'd be starting from. I checked the mats—not bad. I went to the pommel horse, and was surprised to see a bizarre covering on it. The top of the leathery horse should be firm and sticky so your hands don't slide; the sides should be smooth and slippery so your legs can swing freely. This one had two different materials on it—the sides were leather but the top was some type of synthetic and looked as if it might be slippery. Better be careful on that one.

The parallel bars, rings and high bar seemed pretty much like what I was used to. No problem.

I went to the vault last, and touched it to test the tension. It bounced back. It was a spring horse, unlike any we used in the United States. I'd had very limited exposure on one, but knew it was actually better with the springs. It made for a bouncier surface that lets you get higher in the air. I thought this would be a positive situation for me, and, for once, I actually looked forward to the vault.

This finished, I would now be able to visualize my routines exactly as I would perform them, in the right setting, with the right surroundings. I left the arena and went to register.

While I was picking up my free T-shirt, sports bag and the usual pile of goodies that awaited us at every meet, the other guys arrived at the complex: Scott Johnson, Dan Hayden, Charlie Lakes, Tom Schlesinger and my hometown neighbor, Curtis Holdsworth, who had made his first World team. Our alternates, John Omori and Colin Godkin, came with them: Colin was to be my roommate this time around.

"Where's the arena?" Scott asked. He knew me well. He knew I would have already scoped out the place.

We got our schedule and returned to our hotel: we were to begin training that night in the training gym adjacent to the hotel. The hotel was typically European: old and modest. It even had an outdated elevator which featured a tiny round window that enabled you to watch the floors as they churned by.

Our room was very dark, a disappointment to me because I had only recently begun reading for pleasure. All the times on the road while I was still in school I had always been armed with textbooks; now I didn't like to travel without a Stephen King thriller. The first thing I did in the room was position a chair beside the window, where I'd be able to read in comfort.

The book I had with me was *Misery*—an edge-of-the-chair tale of a famous writer who, after a car accident that shattered his legs, had been kidnapped by one of his fans, a madwoman, and tortured—a torture that included chopping off one foot with an ax. It was pretty spine-tingling—just the kind of story I liked to get my blood pumping and my adrenaline high for competition.

We had a week to train before the competition was to begin. Each morning was much the same: we'd have breakfast—a huge buffet that featured European favorites like yogurt, fruit, cereal, eggs and fish (yuck, I *hate* fish!). As for me, I brought along my peanut butter. This was no time to start eating a big breakfast.

We worked out from ten-thirty until noon; by the time we changed and got back to our hotel it was two o'clock—too late for lunch, but we were hungry.

"There's a McDonald's across the street!" Scott announced on the second day. We were saved!

Our next training session was at six, and after that it was dinner back at the hotel. After a few days I began to feel the security of the routine; it was one more way of preparing me for competition.

The major talk buzzing around the arena was, thankfully, not about me. It was about Dmitri Bilozerchev.

"He's *back*!" was the word.

"How is that possible?"

"Amazing!"

I saw him after one of the workouts and had a chance to talk with him briefly. Seeing him gave me the confidence to disregard any soreness I might be feeling in my neck; my glance automatically went to his leg, to the gruesome purple scar, which made me cringe. Later I watched him warming up. It was obvious his leg wasn't great; he was doing very little tumbling and vaulting and was rolling out of his dismounts, the scar on the inside of his calf seeming to pulsate with every turn. It really *was* amazing that he was back.

Between workouts we were on our own. We found a laundromat (at long last—there hadn't been one in West Germany) and when I went there one afternoon I found myself laughing at the absurdity of it all. Here I was, competing on the U.S. World Team at the World Championships, but, God, I still had to have clean clothes! There are some things even being a celebrity cannot change. It was humbling.

But even in the steamy laundromat or out on the street flecked with cozy shops and warm bakeries, the purpose of being there never left my mind. Its level of intensity changed, but it was always there, like a constant hum in my brain. I'd walk along the street, not realizing the hum was there, when suddenly I'd look up and see a sign for "Ahoi Arena," where the competition was to be held. The hum would increase in decibels, quickly becoming a loud buzz of anticipation.

"Oh, yeah, the World Championships," I said aloud, whenever this happened.

At last, the meet was to begin. We walked in, the first night of competition—the compulsories—and the arena was packed with people. Mary Lou Retton and Bart Conner were there; they would be doing the commentating at the 1988 Olympics for NBC. This was "practice" for them, to get them familiar with the routine of broadcasting. It was no longer practice for me, it was business.

I made it through all the compulsory events and did fairly well, even managing to put in a decent ring routine, the biggest concern since I'd ruptured the disc in my neck. I ended up in medal contention on the vault and high bar, and was well situated in the All-Around standings.

We had a day off between the competition, and I rested. The next day I felt great—better than I had in a long, long time.

The first event of the optionals was the floor. I did a double layout and did it well—apparently my ankles were going to survive. Next was the horse; I did well there, too, and got a good score. Then it was time for rings, and I was nervous about my optional routine, I hit it right. My left side was working! This was the last charge I needed—now I knew I could do it, I could do anything. I was actually in the lead for the U.S. Men. My success on rings really psyched me. Now I had a chance to make the finals.

One of my ankles, however, got a little tender after my dismount from the rings. I wrapped more tape around it and prepared for the next event, vaulting.

I had gotten a 9.8 on the compulsory vault. The competitor before me got a 9.75 and had taken a step on his landing. I knew if I could do it perfectly, I would get a much higher score and, combined with my 9.8, I would make the finals, no problem. Vaulting had never been one of my favorite events: to win a medal in it at the World Championships would be a real milestone in my career.

I was going to do a skill called the "Piked Cuervo"—one I had performed countless times before. It would be easy. I'd nail it. No problem. And I'd show the world that, once and for all, Tim Daggett was back. Tim Daggett was a Champion.

I saluted the judge, thinking, *This is going to be my ultimate comeback, my ultimate triumph.*

I ran down the runway, hit the board and exploded with power and force like I hadn't done in years. I flew higher than I'd gone before . . . further from the vault, more thrilling than ever before. I did a half twist and a perfect pike . . . but, somehow, I got a little bit crooked in the air, came down a little bit off, and, upon impact, heard what sounded like a rifle shot explode throughout the arena.

"What the hell was that?" I asked myself. I knew I'd been hurt, and in an instant I scanned my body to see what had happened. First I looked at my right leg. It was intact. Then I looked at my left: I saw my tibia sticking out about six inches, the jagged ridges of bone clearly visible through the translucent skin. My first reaction was to grab the bone and pull it back into my leg before it broke through the skin. The pain followed quickly. I rolled onto my side and screamed "God!"

Mary Lou was on the other side of the arena. She later told reporters she heard that same rifle-shot sound, and knew right away it was the sound of breaking bones. Others must have heard the sound, too, for suddenly, the arena became eerily quiet.

Our trainer, Jack Rockwell, was in the stands. He flew over the wall and dropped to the floor. It's a wonder he didn't break his leg, too.

Suddenly, there was pandemonium all around me.

"Ice! Ice!" someone shouted. It sounded like Yefim.

"Get him off the floor, *fast!*"

"It's swelling! My god, it's already swelling!"

Flashbulbs exploded in my face. I hurt. God, how I hurt.

"Where the hell is the ice?"

"He's going into shock!" a woman shouted.

No. No. I didn't want to be unconscious. I tried to tell her I was okay. The sounds and shouts became a blur, and the next thing I knew I was strapped onto a stretcher and carried off the competition floor, juggled through what seemed like crowds of people hovering over me, staring, their hands clamped over their mouths. The pain was rapidly increasing. Now I almost wished I could pass out. Anything. Anything to make the pain go away.

They brought me into the medical facilities at the arena. A blood pressure band was strapped around my arm. A pill was shoved down my throat.

"Cut off the wrist wraps!" someone yelled.

"*NO!*" It was Yefim. "He'll need those again. I'll take them off." Yefim knew of my sentimental attachment to those wraps, but at that point I hardly cared if they were cut. But *he* cared, and he quickly, carefully, removed them.

An IV was stuck into my hand. My leg was swelling more and more as each second, each minute, passed. I tried to turn it: there was a strange, grinding sound. And pain. More pain. There were so many people: I remember seeing faces, though their words became unclear, melting into one another. Yefim was there. Abie. Jack. My manager, Nancy.

"Make them stop the tape! Make them stop it!"

I realized there was a monitor in the room. The broadcasters were playing and replaying my fall. Yefim looked as if he was going to be sick.

"Hospital's been notified," I heard clearly.

"We're on the way!"

I was picked up again and rushed through the halls.

Jack rode with me in the ambulance.

"It's okay, Tim, it's okay. You're going to be okay," he kept repeating, as if to convince himself.

Somewhere in the distant night I heard the muffled sound of sirens and saw the flashing glare of red lights. I wondered if there was an accident up ahead; then I realized that the sirens and lights were coming from the ambulance I was in.

I was in and out of reality, but I remember feeling rage. It wasn't fair! After all I'd been through with my neck! Then another emotion crept in—something I never revealed to the press, something I never even told my coach, my friends or my family—I felt relief. Finally, my battle was over . . . finally my body had won out over my mind, and, at last, the struggle was gong to end.

17

O nce inside the hospital, there was more chaos. Doctors were everywhere, shouting at one another in a language I couldn't understand. I was taken into a curtained-off area and a mask was put over my mouth, my nose.

"Nitrous oxide," Jack said. "It will help the pain."

It didn't.

Two of the doctors spoke English. They fired questions at me.

"Can you move ankle?"

"Can you wiggle toes?"

"Does it hurt?"

Does it hurt?

I was vaguely aware of others fumbling around my leg. I couldn't understand the commotion. By now I figured I had broken my leg. So what's the big deal? Just set it and get me out of here. I did not know my leg was swelling to balloon proportions; I did not know that an artery had been severed, and my leg was filling with runaway blood.

Another doctor appeared at my side.

"Tim, Tim can you hear me?" he asked in broken English.

I looked at him, thinking I couldn't speak through the mask.

"Tim!" the doctor raised his voice with urgency.

"We need a reaction from him!" another voice shouted.

"Tim!"

"Is he going out?"

"Tim!"

I struggled to open my eyes. I looked into a swirling sea of faces above me.

"Tim, we have to open you up."

I reached up and ripped off the mask. I turned to my trainer.

"Jack, don't let them cut me over here! I want to go home. We'll have it done there."

The doctor understood me and said, simply and clearly, "Well, then, my son, you will lose your leg."

They prepared me for surgery. Jack assured me he would be in the operating room. I felt the sting of a shot; another mask was snapped over my face; I saw Yefim's face, then Nancy's.

How did they get to the hospital? I wondered. Then I thought about the competition.

"Go back, go back," I said to Yefim. "The guys . . . they need you . . ."

Then I closed my eyes and let myself slowly sink into the welcomed darkness . . .

I was sick. I felt myself wake up, aware that it was morning. My stomach heaved. Then there was pain. I opened my eyes and looked down. My leg was still there. They had not amputated. I put my head back on my pillow.

Moments—or hours—later I awoke again. Nancy was there, saying something to me.

"Who won?" I remember asking.

She smiled. "Dmitri."

Wow. Incredible. Dmitri Bilozerchev had won the World Championships on a chewed-up leg. Leg. I looked down again. It was still there. I went out again.

I heard faraway voices. I opened my eyes. It was a stranger's face. " . . . stay here . . . a couple of weeks . . ." his voice was saying.

"What?" I asked. This seemed important.

"You can't go home." His words became clearer. "You have to stay here a while."

"Where's the team?" My voice was a whisper.

"Gone. Gone home."

I drifted off. The nightmares began. Suddenly I became Stephen King's character. A celebrity. A mangled leg. Kidnapped. Held hostage. Trapped. They were going to cut off my leg. I woke myself up, screaming inside.

Nancy was there. "We weren't about to leave you alone," she said.

I went back to sleep.

You won't make me mad again, will you?" It was Annie, the madwoman from the book. She stood over my bed with an ax. I woke up crying. I vomited.

They had to change the bandages. Two doctors were there. Two nurses.

"I want you to look at this," one doctor said.

I thought he was talking to the others.

He looked me in the eye. I turned away.

"You, Tim. I want you to look at your leg."

"No," I said.

"You must."

"What?"

"You must look at your leg. You must learn to deal with it. It looks wonderful. It's healing nicely."

I looked at my leg. It was huge, swollen. It did not look like a leg at all. There was a huge, gaping hole, about eight inches long and four inches wide. It was blood red. I saw purple muscles. I saw globs of fat tissue. There was no skin: only a raw, open wound. It looked like an animal lying in the road, hit by a car, its guts spilling out of its sides. I vomited.

I could not eat. Each day I could almost feel my bones protruding more, could almost sense muscle deteriorating, strength leaving my body. I cried. All my hard work. And now, now this. This pain.

I looked down at my leg. There was a pin sticking out of my heel. How did that get there? I drifted back to sleep, back to Annie wielding her ax.

A doctor was at my bedside.

"How do you feel?"

His words woke me. "Pain," I muttered.

"You've just had your shot. It will ease quickly now."

I was having morphine every three hours. The numbness it provided lasted only two.

"I'd like to tell you about your surgery," he continued.

"No." All I could visualize was the bloody, purple mass.

He ignored me. "We performed what is called a 'fasciotomy.' We had to repair the severed artery, then set the bone in place. You lost a lot of blood—five and a half pints. But we saved your leg. You were lucky."

Lucky? He called this "luck"?

"You will be going home soon."

Now he had my full attention.

"When?"

"Another week. We still have to remove the pin and put a cast on before you leave."

I went back to sleep. This time I sprang from the vault, flew through the air. I landed, a crumpled heap. I grabbed my leg. The pain. The pain. Annie was standing over me. *"You won't make me mad again, will you?"*

The days stretched on. Once I awoke to see Nancy in my room and several other faces I didn't know. Nurses. Doctors. All the people who had come to look at the freak. Most of them couldn't speak English. They jabbered to each other, talking about me, saying frightful things.

I could tell by the tone of their voices. I guess the painkillers, combined with depression, were wreaking havoc with my mind.

"How're you doing?" Nancy said quietly, trying to reassure me.

"Okay," I answered. I didn't want to talk. I didn't want to look at her. I still couldn't look Nancy or anyone in the eye. I was too ashamed, too angry with myself, too angry with God.

Just then another stranger entered the room. I noticed he was smiling. It seemed like an eternity since I'd seen anyone smile.

"Mr. Tim Daggett, I have something for you!" he exclaimed, beaming, then reached into his jacket pocket.

He thrust a picture in my face. It was me. Lying on the floor of the arena, my face screaming in pain, my leg twisted and deformed, the bone sticking out clearly.

I cried out.

Nancy grabbed the picture from his hand.

"Good god, are you sick?" she shouted at him. "Get out! *Get out!*"

"But it ran in all big European papers! A great picture, no?"

"No!" she shouted. "Get out!" She forced him out the door.

A few days later they told me I was going home. But first, the surgery to remove the pin, to put on the cast. I couldn't wait. I was going home.

The morning after the surgery I awoke in tremendous pain. And I was sick again. How much longer? I looked down at my leg and saw the safety of the rough white cast. No more gaping wound, no more gore. But the pain, oh, the pain. Would it ever go away?

I drifted in and out of sleep all day, waking up only when the nightmares came, only when the morphine wore off. I thought about Peter. I thought about Mitch. All the years they had done gymnastics, neither of them had ever been seriously injured. Most people never were. Why me? Why again? But this time I would not be fighting to do the sport I loved . . . the fight ahead of me was to save my leg.

Late into the night I awoke to a bolt of pain shooting through my leg. I could feel a throbbing, pounding, pressurelike pain from within the cast, as though my leg wanted to explode from the plaster. I snapped on the light and looked down, not expecting to see anything. Blood had begun to seep through the porous white casting material, outlining the gaping wounds. I sensed a pressure building within the cast; with it, the pain grew worse.

Below the cast, my toes poked out of the end. I could see them clearly. They were blue. I touched them. They were ice. My god. My leg is dying. I thought I was going to go insane.

I rang for the nurse, who came quickly.

"I need the doctor!" I said, trying to stay calm.

She smiled. "Doctor will be here at seven o'clock," she said, proud of her ability to understand some English.

"I cannot take the pain. It's getting worse. My toes are blue." I pointed to my toes, but she looked at me and smiled again. I realized she had no idea what I was talking about. "Please, call the doctor. DOCTOR! He must come NOW!"

She smiled again, unable to understand the magnitude of my terror.

"Doctor will be here at seven o'clock," she repeated. She left the room.

I glanced at the clock. It was 3:00 A.M. I became overwhelmed with anxiety. *Why didn't anyone understand me?* Why did this have to happen *here*? Why couldn't it have happened where they at least spoke my language? The last words I remembered hearing from the doctor were "You will lose your leg." *God, no one had yet said the danger was over.* But though I had wanted someone to tell me I'd be all right, now, I knew they'd be lying. I was going to lose my leg. I just knew it.

Then I did the only thing I could think of. I started screaming, and I didn't stop. Not until the doctor arrived at my bedside several minutes later.

"Well . . ." he said slowly. "What have we here?"

I stared at him, unable to talk.

"Looks like the cast is much too tight," he said nonchalantly. "We'll have to do something about this, won't we?"

He cracked the edge of the cast and it suddenly split open all the way to the top. Immediately I felt the pressure subside. I looked down and saw that the crack was about one inch wide. No wonder I had so much pain. The leg was swollen and the circulation had stopped.

"In the morning we'll plaster over the seam," the doctor said. "Now get some rest." He turned off the light and left.

I stared at the dark ceiling, trying to think. The doctor had still not told me my leg was going to be fine. I felt an ache in my gut. I needed reassurance. I needed comforting. I thought of my mom, then I pushed the thought from my mind. I couldn't afford to think of her now. I needed her here too badly.

The next morning before they replastered my cast they took me for an X-ray. The orderlies didn't speak English; I silently let them wheel my bed to the lab. They left me there with two X-ray technicians. They didn't speak English, either. But it was apparent to me they were going to have to move me to a table under the machine.

Quickly, one of them grasped my shoulders; the other went to grab my ankles. I screamed.

"Are you crazy? You can't pick me up by my ankles!" they looked at me, stunned. "You get another person in here *immediately!*"

They got the message. I couldn't wait to get home.

Nancy made all the arrangements for the flight home. I had no idea until much later how complicated this all was. I just did as I was told, and patiently let them strap me to the stretcher that took me to the ambulance. As we went through the hospital doors, one of the paramedics slipped. He almost dropped me. I remained calm, crying on the inside.

It was to be a direct, nonstop flight from Rotterdam to Los Angeles. The doctors gave Nancy enough morphine pills to sustain me through the long flight.

Inside the plane was frightening. Several seats had been removed and a narrow bed installed. Around the bed were curtains; at least I would have some privacy; I wouldn't have to look at the other passengers. All the way home I kept thinking about them. What kind of freak must they think is behind the curtains? Every so often a little turbulence would cause the curtains to flutter and a crack of light appeared. My god, they can see in! I closed my eyes. Nancy peeked in a few times to check on me, and to give me my pills. Were the other passengers watching? I wasn't usually this paranoid—maybe it was the morphine, maybe it was the pain.

I fought sleep, not wanting to awaken with a screaming nightmare. Not wanting Annie to be on the plane. I only wanted to be home. Home.

"Last one," Nancy announced as she poked her head through the curtains and gave me another morphine pill. "We'll be in L.A. in three hours."

Three hours. I could make it. I could make it.

We finally arrived, and began circling the airport. And circling. And circling. Suddenly, the pilot's voice came over the intercom.

"Due to severe weather, LAX has been closed. We're diverting to Las Vegas until the storm passes. Sorry for the delay. We hope this won't be too much of an inconvenience."

I heard the other passengers groan. I just lay there, looking at the ceiling. The effects of the last morphine pill were starting to wear off. The pain was returning. "My god," I thought, "this is never going to end."

We landed in Las Vegas. There were no customs facilities there, and because this was an international flight, no one was allowed to leave or enter the plane. The pain grew worse.

I tried to sleep; I no longer cared if Annie returned. After about an hour and a half, the pilot announced that LAX had reopened and we were leaving. I didn't believe him until I heard the engines rev and felt the plane begin to taxi.

I have never felt a more welcome sensation than the squeal of the tires as we touched down in Los Angeles. Home. My god, I was home.

They took me off the plane and put me into an ambulance right away—I never did go through customs. Nancy stayed behind to check everything through.

"Please . . . hurry . . ." was all I could say to the paramedics.

The sirens screamed once again; the red lights flashed. When I finally saw the familiar outline of the UCLA Medical Center, I let the tears come.

They rushed me into the emergency room and I looked up to see the most wonderful sight of all. There, standing over me, was my brother Michael.

18

Beside Michael was another familiar face: Dr. Mandelbaum. "Welcome home, Tim," he said.

That's when I realized I didn't have my insurance card.

"Oh, my god!" I freaked out. "I can't get in!"

"What are you talking about?" Michael asked.

"They won't let me in the hospital! My blue card is in my wallet—Nancy has it!"

Dr. Mandelbaum laughed. "Don't worry, Tim, I'll vouch for you."

He took me into a room, checked me out and did some tests. I finally got a long-awaited shot of morphine. It was after midnight when he finished. Then he gave me the news.

"Well, Tim, we've gone over all your tests. You've been one lucky guy."

There was that word again.

"Here's the story. First of all, we have to remove the cast, reset your leg and attach an external fixator."

"What's that?"

He smiled. "Well, it's pretty funny-looking, but it will do the trick."

He explained that the fixator was a large appliance of black metal. Just under my knee there would be a thick arc which would be raised about six inches from the surface and wrap around almost to the back of my leg; two side pieces would run down the length of my leg on either side and connect across the bottom of my foot; in the front of my leg, three long metal rods would connect to the top piece and be drilled into my bone, then run the length of my shin and be drilled again, into the bone at the top of my foot. It sounded pretty scary.

"How long will I need it?" I asked.

"A while. Several weeks. And there's something else. Later we're going to have to graft some skin to cover the wounds."

A skin graft? I'd somehow thought they'd be able to stitch me up and I'd be as good as new. Visions of Dmitri's purple scar came to mind.

"Also, you've got to eat."

"I don't feel like eating. I feel sick."

"Timmy," he got real serious now. "You've lost twenty-five pounds. You're malnourished. We don't need any more complications than we already have."

Twenty-five pounds? Wow. I must really be skinny. Add that to the ten pounds I had dropped just before the World Championships to be as light as possible . . . wow . . . I only weighed 110 pounds.

They performed the surgery that night. When I woke the next morning I looked at my leg. I felt a dulled fear, then slid back into the safety of sleep. Most of that morning I drifted in and out of sleep, of consciousness, vaguely aware each time I awoke of a grotesque appliance surrounding my leg. When I finally came to with a fuzzy sense of reality, the shock of seeing what was now part of my leg gripped me with horror.

"What the hell is that?" I said aloud. Although Dr. Mandelbaum had tried to prepare me for that godawful thing, I don't think anything could have prepared me. It looked like something that belonged to Darth Vader. The momentary happiness I'd had in being home quickly faded, and I sank back into a deep depression.

The following day I was back in the operating room for the skin graft. They sliced off about a six-by-ten-inch patch of skin from my hip and punched holes in the skin to allow it to stretch, so they wouldn't have to take as much. They affixed the patch to my wounds: the eight-by-four-inch one on the outside of my calf; the four-by-two-inch one on the inside. They bandaged the areas, and the next morning the bandages had to come off. God, it hurt. I looked at the wounds: they were no longer huge, gaping holes; now they looked like my grand-mother's patchwork quilt, woven with little dots of dried blood where the stitches would have been.

I had left my nightmares of Annie behind on the plane, but new, equally frightening ones surfaced. Whenever I closed my eyes I saw myself in a gym, falling over and over again from every piece of apparatus, breaking my leg over and over, feeling the pain as vividly as if it were real.

It seemed I was never alone. Between the doctors and nurses fussing over me, cleaning the wounds, checking my progress, cleaning the holes where the metal rods went in, there was always someone coming or going from my room. Michael was there every day, and after a few days, Dr. Mandelbaum let me have visitors. I did not want to see anyone; he didn't care. He let them come anyway, though later I learned that he had stopped the press from coming, and allowed only my friends to be there. He felt it would be good for my spirit. It wasn't.

Coach Shurlock, the head coach of UCLA, arrived one day with frozen yogurt for me. I had just had a shot and my stomach was doing flips. There was no way I could eat it.

"You have to!" he said. "Dr. Mandelbaum told me to bring it!"

It was then I discovered that Dr. Mandelbaum had called my friends and pleaded with them to bring food to me when they came—things they knew I liked. It was his way of trying to get me to eat! Unfortu-nately, the pile of Mrs. Fields cookies, M&M's and other goodies just collected dust on my nightstand.

Peter and Donna came, Mitch came, Mark and Yefim came. The girls on the UCLA Women's Gymnastics Team came, too, and one of them, Carrie O'Connor, brought me a most appropriate gift—a four-leaf clover. I still carry it pressed between plastic wrap in my wallet.

Through it all, I was ashamed. I was embarrassed and humiliated. I couldn't stand looking at the faces of everyone when they came into my room for the first time—the sight of my skeletal, prone body and the ghastly fixator drilled into my leg startled them, and I hated watching them try to regain their composure. I wondered what I had looked like before when I'd seen a person with a deformity. I became ashamed of myself for that, too. It was a vicious, never-ending cycle.

One day Mitch's brother Chuck stopped by. He later told me that though the guys had told him to "be prepared," nothing could have explained how grotesque I looked. He said he wanted to turn and run out the door, but it was too late, I had already seen him. I had already supposed that was the way most people were reacting, and it bothered me. If it had been one of my friends lying there, I don't know how I would have handled it.

One day they decided to X-ray my leg. I had also been having chest pains, which they felt was from the buildup of fluid in my lungs from three weeks of lying in bed. Until then, I hadn't even been able to sit up.

I was wheeled in the bed to X-ray, where a very frail, petite oriental woman was going to do them. She positioned my leg under the machine—that was fine, no problem. But for my chest she needed to have me stand.

"That might be a problem," I told her.

"Don't worry, just hold on to me."

Great. I slid off the side of the bed and put my good foot on the floor. Instantly, the room started spinning and I immediately passed out, slumping against her, pushing her against the wall. I came to and yelled at her.

"*I told you not to make me stand up! I told you! Didn't I tell you?*" I screamed at her, nearly hysterical. Between the drugs and the entire ordeal, I lost my patience easily now. I was a changed person, and I didn't care.

When Michael came to see me that night, that was all I could talk about.

"She made me stand up! The idiot made me stand up!" I couldn't get it out of my mind.

"She was only doing her job, Tim," he tried to console me, so I got angry at him.

He changed the subject. "I do have some news you might like to hear," he said.

"I doubt it." God, I was turning into a nasty person.

He ignored my comment. "Mom will be here tomorrow. I'll be leaving and she'll be coming. She's planning on staying two weeks."

I wanted to cry, I was so happy. But there was so much anger inside me, so much pain, the tears could no longer get through.

I couldn't believe how strong my mother was. She came with her sister, Alma, and I didn't care if my mother talked to me or did anything to help me. Just having her in the room, sitting beside me, was all the comfort I needed. She was so brave, so accepting of the monstrosity around my leg; I never saw her wince with pain or pull back from disgust. I realize now, however, that I also never saw her after she left my room. Maybe she fell apart then, I don't know. All I know was that I finally found some peace with her there.

Dr. Mandelbaum decided it was time to get me doing things. He wanted me to start therapy to regain my upper body strength.

"Why?" I asked him flatly.

"Because I know you, Timmy. I know you'll want to get back into shape."

"For what? I'll never do gymnastics again. The doctors in Rotterdam told me."

"Just do it, that's all. Doctor's orders." God, he was making me crazy. I felt like I wanted to put my fist through the wall.

But Dr. Mandelbaum *did* know me. I don't think he would have taken the same approach with every patient, but he knew my commitment to the sport. He also knew it was the only thing that might get me out of that depression.

Zack tried to work with me. I fought it all the way. I didn't want physical therapy. I wanted to be left alone. I must have been a real joy to be around. My body had betrayed me—gymnastics had betrayed me—and I wanted no part of any of it. Deep down I had always felt that if I worked hard I could accomplish anything . . . now I saw this philosophy as a major flaw in my character. I must have been a jerk to believe that. Talk about naive.

Finally, they said I could go home.

"But not until you can clean the openings around the rods yourself," the nurse said emphatically. Gross as it was, I learned how to do it in a hurry.

After a long, foggy month, I was finally off the morphine—at last I could think clearly again!—and had regained some weight. But being in a hospital for over a month had taken its toll on me. When they wheeled me into my apartment, I felt as though I'd never been there before.

I had nurses twenty-four hours a day, and my mom and Aunt Alma stayed another week. When they had to leave, I acted like a two-year-old.

"Don't leave, Mom. Please don't leave me." I cried.

But she did have to go. She had six kids and a job waiting for her. It must really have hurt her to see me become so childish.

Dr. Mandelbaum checked up on me every day. "Are you doing your therapy?"

"Yes," I lied.

I decided I wanted to see a movie. I coerced the nurse into taking me. Once we were in the theater, I was sorry I had come. Getting in and out of the wheelchair to get into the car with that bulky, hideous contraption was difficult enough, but inside, the nurse opened the door for me while she went to get popcorn. I told her I'd be fine, and started to move the wheelchair down the sloping aisle. It slipped and got away from me. I slid down the aisle until the chair plowed into a row of seats, my Darth Vader leg sticking up in the air, nearly ending up in someone's face. People stared.

"I'm an invalid!" I wanted to scream. "I can't even go to a stupid movie!" I was beginning to have a monopoly on self-pity.

Slowly, slowly, my body started to respond. With the drugs out of my system, I had stopped being sick. My leg still had a long way to go—I certainly couldn't even think about doing gymnastics again—but my mind had an even greater struggle ahead. Waking up every morning took on new meaning: how was I going to get through the day?

Thanksgiving was quickly approaching. Peter had called, and invited me for dinner. I didn't want to go. He and Donna lived nearly sixty miles from L.A., and I was sure I wasn't up to the trip. Besides that, I didn't want to ruin their holiday. How could I not? What pleasure could they have with a depressed, burdensome lump of a human being who needed constant care intruding on their good time?

In the end, my mother convinced me to go. Each day she called. Then one of my brothers called. Then one of my sisters called. They all said the same thing: "Go to Peter's."

The day arrived. My nurse packed me in the car and we began the journey. I was so irrational, so within myself, I'd thought that because it was Thanksgiving, traffic would be light. After a few minutes on the freeway, I saw otherwise.

"We're gong to be late!" I screamed at the nurse.

"No, Tim," she patiently tried to reassure me. "We'll be fine."

I pictured Peter's family sitting around, waiting for me, waiting for this invalid to come and ruin their day.

"Turn the car around!" I shouted. "Turn it around! We're going back! I can't do this!"

"You'll be fine," the nurse said quietly.

I wanted to go home. I wanted to reach over, grab the wheel and make her stop. But, once again, I was reminded of my helplessness.

My life was no longer in my hands; other people made my decisions now, and I was at their mercy.

By the time we arrived, I was exhausted.

Peter's parents and some of his sisters were there, as were Donna's parents. I was still embarrassed by the way my leg looked, but they all tried very hard to put me at ease. Little Timothy was now two years old, and chattering a string of nonstop, jumbled words. I thought he would be afraid of my Darth Vader outfit—he acted as though it wasn't even there. I guess you never know about kids!

Halfway through dinner I was so tired I could no longer sit.

"You know, man," I said to Peter, "I think I'd better lie down a while."

Everyone got out of the way and I lay on the floor. It was actually pretty funny—me on the floor, with all Peter's relatives standing over me holding a conversation with me, like this was nothing unusual, and a strange nurse sitting at his dining room table eating a turkey dinner.

It was a tiring day, but by the time I got home, I was glad I had gone. For the first time since my injury I had, if only for a few hours, stopped focusing solely on myself. Thankful? Yeah, I was thankful on this Thanksgiving Day if for nothing else than to have a friend like Peter.

How or why Dr. Mandelbaum and Zack put up with me remains a mystery. They simply didn't quit. Outside my apartment the street sloped down a hill. Every day, Zack wanted me to wheel down the hill, then back up. I humored him. I went down with no problem. But there was no way I was going to try to get back up. Why should I? I made the nurse push me.

And then one day, something happened. The nurse took me outside for my daily "wheel" and I spontaneously made a decision.

"I'm going to make it up the hill alone today, no matter what," I told her. "I want no help. Don't catch the chair if I start to slide back. I mean it. I really mean it."

There was never any thought that accomplishing this was going to get me ready for the Olympic Trials. The only thing I could focus on was making it up that hill.

The chair was hard to control. I was weak; my arms had little strength. But I pushed and I pushed. I slid back.

The nurse obeyed my orders. She left me alone. The chair was resisting me, but I could do it. I kept pushing, kept sliding back. I was Sylvester Stallone in *Rocky*, pushing to make my way up those steps, pushing to prove to myself I could do it. Pushing, pushing. My arms strained, my jaw tightened. Almost there. Almost there. Suddenly, I was at the top of the hill. I had made it. And I felt better than I had in a long, long time. This was my first realization that I could, after all, have a goal that didn't include gymnastics. It was my first indication that my mind was beginning to heal. Now, like Rocky, I was ready for the fight.

Out of the bad often comes some good. Or so they say, whoever "they" are. Well, if nothing else, each time I went outside my apartment I no longer had to worry about autograph seekers coming up to me: if a person ever wants to feel anonymous, he should have Dr. Mandelbaum fix him up with one of these things. It's so scary-looking, people actually cross the street so they don't have to look at you!

Mike Chaplain was my roommate at the time, and he gradually began hinting that I maybe would want to go to the gym.

The *gym*? Was he *crazy*? That was the last place I wanted to go. I figured that Dr. Mandelbaum and Zack were putting him up to it. It was bad enough that I had to watch Mike leave every day, knowing where he was going—that he was going to *that place* to *work out*. I didn't want to hear anything about it.

One night he came home and said, "Tim, the guys have been asking about you. They really want to see you. Think about coming over to the gym. That's all I'm going to say about it."

I put the thought of the gym behind me and started thinking about the guys. They were my friends. We'd all been through a lot together over the years. I was worried about Curtis Holdsworth; I knew after I broke my leg he was the next man up for the United States. I hoped that watching what happened to me hadn't messed him up. I was afraid it had. Mike was right. I really should go see the guys.

The next day I had the nurse pack me in the car again, this time to take me to the gym.

I wheeled directly into the training room. Charlie Lakes was there: he'd not yet seen the addition to my leg.

"Holy mackerel!" he screamed. "What the hell is that?"

It broke the ice.

I wheeled from the training room and headed across campus, past Pauley Pavilion, toward the John Wooden Center. Along the way, I was conscious of kids walking to classes, stepping aside to let me pass, with horrified looks on their faces and murmurs passed between them. I stared straight ahead.

But once at the gym, I wheeled through the doors. I saw Mike standing with his back toward me. Then, for the first time since the injury, I let go of the depression. I positioned my chair directly behind Mike and pushed myself forward. I aimed for my target and hit it head—or rather, leg—on, bumping Mike's back with my elevated leg. He turned quickly.

"It's about time," he laughed.

Later he told me it was at that moment that he knew I was going to be all right.

On December 20, I went back to the hospital to have the fixator removed. Good-bye Darth Vader. Good riddance.

I had actually been working on my upper body, with no intentions, but just doing it out of habit.

"You're going to make it back, Tim," Dr. Mandelbaum said, as he prepared me for this, my fifth surgery.

I still wasn't ready to hear that.

With the monstrosity removed, Dr. Mandelbaum told me he wanted to hook me up to a bone stimulator, a small device that they would

place under the cast to electronically pulsate the bone, hopefully quick-
ening the healing process. There was no proof that it would help. "But
it can't hurt," he said. "And it may buy you some time."

"Time for what?" I asked.

He smiled. "Well, you know the Olympic Trials aren't that far
away."

I could have kicked him, but I didn't want to risk hurting my one
good leg.

Two days later, with a normal-looking cast, hobbling on normal-
looking crutches, I did what I wanted to do more than anything in the
world: I flew home for Christmas.

19

It was the most wonderful Christmas I can remember. I am so lucky to have such a big, caring family and so many, many friends. With the holiday cheer and the spirit of the season all around me, my mind took on a new dimension—happiness.

I considered staying in West Springfield; it would have been the easy thing to do. But then, I didn't want to have to get a new doctor, and after living in L.A. for nearly eight years, almost everything I owned was out there. It would be such a hassle to stay. But for now, for these two weeks, it was heaven.

One night, after a whole gang had been to the house, I limped into bed and did some serious thinking. I realized then that, like pushing the wheelchair up the hill, there would be other goals for me in life beside gymnastics. I wanted to be married someday, have a family, own my own house. Until then, there would be other things, too. After tonight I knew that people still cared about me even though I was no longer a star—that they loved me for being me, not for being a gymnast.

I don't know why I felt that way. It had never consciously crossed my mind that I was doing gymnastics to make people love me. I'd always felt secure in the love of my family. But I guess with all I'd been through, this was the kind of reinforcement I needed now. As I lay in bed, I put my life into perspective, and saw me, Tim Daggett. I would be in this life tomorrow and the next day and the next. Gymnastics or not. It was up to me to make the most of my life.

I went back to Los Angeles on January 5. It was 1988, a new year, and I had a new resolve. I was going to get through this with a more positive attitude.

I no longer needed my round-the-clock nurses. That was a step in the right direction. I sat in my living room, then decided to get something to read from the bookcase. The nurses had partially rearranged my apartment in order to make room for all the things they needed, and I wasn't sure what was on the shelf.

I hobbled over to give it a closer look. That's when I saw it. My gymnastics training diary. The one I had kept since I was a little boy. I usually kept it on my nightstand; the nurses must have moved it there, clearly visible, for all the world to see.

Something told me, "Tim, don't go near that! It's too soon—it's from another life!" I guess I knew all along what I would find. But I was drawn to it. I reached up onto the shelf and took it down. I carried it back to the couch, sat down and opened it. There, on the inside front cover, were the words. They were a bit faded, a little bit time-worn, but they were still clearly visible to my heart: *If you give up your dream, you'll die.*

It was then that I knew I would not go out from the sport I loved with my last memories those of being carried out on a stretcher. Gymnastics was too much a part of me, too much a part of my life to give it up before I was ready. It was then that I knew I was going to fight this all the way. I was going to go on, and I was going to be the best that I could be. If that meant not being able to make it to Seoul, so be it. I was going to try. And trying was all that mattered now.

I called Dr. Mandelbaum.

"I'm going back into training. I'm going to try for Seoul," I told him.

There was silence on the other end of the line.

"I'll be with you all the way, Tim," he finally said, "only if you promise to work closely with Zack. Between the three of us, I think we can make it happen."

I know now that many coaches and gymnasts were critical of Dr. Mandelbaum. Some said he was being too positive. Some said he was giving me false hope. But without his support, I don't think I'd have returned to the gym at all. He knew a positive attitude was going to be an important part of the healing process for me, not so much the physical as the emotional. He knew having a dream was the best thing for me, and he didn't try to discourage me.

Later, of course, when he realized how serious I was about training for Seoul, the roles reversed. Suddenly *he* was the one telling *me* to slow down.

"But you told me I could do it!" I needled him.

"Maybe not quite this way," he said, exasperated.

If Dr. Mandelbaum thought he had seen "The Bull" come to life after my neck injury . . . well, he "hadn't seen nothin' yet." My determination was back, and with it came my commitment to be the best that I could be.

It is amazing what the human body can withstand physically. Just when you think you're totally falling apart, there's always something you can do in gymnastics: if your neck is sore you can work to exhaustion on leg-strength exercises; if you sprain your ankle you can still do the pommel horse—until your arms buckle in exhaustion; and you can concentrate on increasing your upper body strength. As for me, when I first went back to the gym, I rode a stationary bike with one leg. Now *that* took coordination!

And just as I'd done in my freshman year while on crutches, I now looked for ways to maximize those things that I *could* control. With all the medical inroads, electronic enhancers and high-tech advances I'd been subjected to, I still had to go back to the basics if I was to progress.

Basic conditioning. Basic training. And the basic knowledge I'd gained over the years about how my body works. It was the basics that had gotten me to the top before; now they would bring me back.

For the next several months I adhered strictly to the schedule I had worked out with Dr. Mandelbaum and Zack, including a one-and-a-half-hour minimum in therapy each day:

7:45 A.M. to 9:00 A.M.—Workout
9:15 A.M. to 11:00 A.M.—Physical therapy
11:15 A.M. to 12:30 P.M.—Workout
12:30 P.M. to 1:00 P.M.—Lunch
1:00 P.M. to 2:45 P.M.—Nap time!
3:00 P.M. to 7:00 P.M.—Workout

Needless to say, it made for a pretty full day. And then, of course, there was the press. Once they found out I was returning to the gym, they came out of the woodwork, dusting off their "Tim Daggett" files and loading their cameras with plenty of film. Once again, I was back on the front pages of sports sections all over the country, in odd-looking photos showing this intense, possibly a little-bit-crazy guy trying to perform skills with a cast on his leg.

As soon as I made the decision, I called Peter so that I could tell him before he read it in the paper. If he was surprised, his voice didn't give him away.

"Well, man, you don't need to hear this, but if you're going to go on, you're going to do it. It's all or nothing. It's not 'Let's see if I can do it.' It's either 'I'm going to do it,' or 'I'm not going to do it.' And *you* can do it."

Peter was wrong. I *did* need to hear that. All the coaches, friends and reporters in the world could say, "We know you can do it," and it didn't mean diddly. But hearing it from Peter made it real. He knew me so well, not just emotionally, but he knew my gymnastics capabilities, too, and, well, it was the confirmation I needed. If Peter thought I could do it, too, then damn, I really could.

At first I could only do strength moves: handstands, push-ups, iron crosses on the rings. And because I'd lost so much weight, strength and muscle tone, I was starting from ground zero. It was as though I'd never been in a gym in my life.

Through it all, Yefim's patience was remarkable. He had to help me up and help me down from the rings, parallel bars and high bar. My natural instinct to dismount myself was something I had to control constantly. Even getting up onto the horse proved difficult: normally I pushed off the floor with both legs; now I had to remember to do it with only my right leg. It took some getting used to, but I had to remind myself how much it would hurt if I forgot and pushed off with both legs. And it *would* hurt, and hurt badly. I know, because one day I forgot. Ouch.

Was I afraid to fall when I was on the apparatus? Ha! You bet I was! I was terrified. Even though I felt I should have been prepared after what I went through coming back from my neck injury, I wasn't. Not really. Each time I mounted the apparatus it was like playing Russian roulette. I wasn't any less scared the first time, or when I was trying a month later. I felt as though, compared with this, my neck injury had been like stubbing a toe.

I had been asked to do a pregame interview at the Super Bowl, where ABC was doing a live broadcast of "Wide World of Sports." Frank Gifford would be doing the show.

I went to San Diego, arrived at the complex, and took the elevator up to the booth. When I got outside the open doorway, I could hear people talking. I waited there a moment, not wanting to interrupt them. Then I realized they were watching the video of me breaking my leg in Rotterdam. I had never seen the tape.

"Watch this," Frank was saying to a couple of guys. "You're not going to believe this, it's so bad." There was silence as they watched, then they all groaned. "Oh, Oh," Frank said. "This is so terrible. I can't imagine. Look at his face!" Then he, as most people I'm told often did, turned and looked away from the screen. He looked directly into my face.

"Tim!" he said with surprise. "Tim! We were, ah, just, ah, going over . . ." He was embarrassed, but I thought it was funny. I started to laugh.

"Hi, Frank. It's okay, really. It's nice to know I have an effect on people! A real 'Agony of Defeat,' isn't it?"

We laughed together, then reviewed what we were going to do in the interview. They wanted me to do a play-by-play narration of what happened during that vault. I wasn't prepared for this. There was no way I could watch it. When air time arrived, I sat there like a stiff. I saw the beginning of the video on the monitor, saw myself running down the runway. Then I turned away, and gave my play-by-play from memory, counting out the pacing in my mind, knowing the exact moment I had landed, going through the entire vault without looking at the screen.

I was finally able to get off crutches sometime in February. My old roommate Luc was getting married and he asked me to stand up for him. Stand up! Ha! I thought that was pretty funny. I was also secretly thankful that I could.

In March I went to the NCAA Championships in Nebraska—not to compete, but to watch. While I was there, I took advantage of the practice time and worked out. The media was there in full force: network TV stations, the major newspapers, the radio networks. Every spare moment I had was spent talking to one reporter or another. I was pleased that they thought I was newsworthy, but I was disappointed in their coverage: they focused totally on the concept that I was trying for a comeback to make it to Seoul.

"Will you actually be able to make the team?"

"Do you think you have a chance for the gold?"

Not once did they get it—that what had become more important to me was not the medals (I already had those!), but the struggle. Sure I wanted to make it to Seoul. But what I was doing was now for myself, for my inner voice which said I had to finish this career knowing I had given it everything I had, that I had not given up because of one moment of anguish and pain. I was fulfilling the commitment to myself to try, nothing more. It was the trying, not the winning, that I was after. They just didn't get it! It was frustrating.

Back in L.A., I got the go-ahead from Dr. Mandelbaum to start trying to do some dismounts—into a huge foam pit. It was tough: my body was an obstacle course. At first, once I landed, I couldn't get out of the pit without Yefim's help. Normally, someone with a leg injury can compensate by landing on his stomach: I couldn't do that because it was dangerous for my neck. And I still had to be careful of my ankles. I must have been quite a sight to watch.

The first routine I was actually able to complete was the compulsory on the pommel horse. What a feeling. That's when Yefim and I made a decision: I was going to compete on the horse in the upcoming USA/Russia competition to be held in April in Phoenix. This decision was not only to see how my leg would hold up, but more importantly, I wanted to do it to see how *I* would hold up. The pressure of competition was so much greater than working out, I really had no idea how—or if—I would be able to go back into an arena with people and cameras and judges. It would be my only opportunity to take a "dry run" in front of a crowd before the Olympic Trials.

The morning after we arrived in Phoenix, I went to the hotel pool after workout. There was a Jacuzzi there, and I thought it would help my leg loosen up a little. I was now out of the cast, but needed to wear a brace most of the time.

I limped out of the pool area, where several other gymnasts were relaxing. On my way to the Jacuzzi, I passed someone talking to a reporter. I looked up. My stomach tightened. It was Dmitri.

I had known he'd be at the meet, and I was looking forward to seeing him again. But running into him this way, so unexpectedly, I wasn't prepared. Dmitri is one of the greatest gymnasts who has ever lived, and as I stood there, face-to-face, the pain he had overcome became very real. "They" had written him off, too, not so long ago. They had told him he shouldn't even try. Now he was the Champion of the

World. Whatever respect and admiration I'd had for him before, now became even greater.

I felt a tingling in my leg, and, as if sensing that, Dmitri smiled and gestured to it, a questioning look on is face.

"It's okay, okay," I said, raising a thumb. I kept walking toward the Jacuzzi, not wanting to interrupt his interview, and, more than that, wanting to regain my composure. I took off my brace to go into the water. A few seconds later, Dmitri was at my side with his interpreter. I looked up, directly into his scar—the scar that had seemed so grotesque only two years before now paled beside my ugly, purple leg.

He looked at my leg. He took a step back.

"Pretty gross, isn't it?" I said.

We talked for a while through his interpreter, and Dmitri showed me some exercises that had helped him through his rehabilitation. It was an odd feeling—I had to keep pushing the emotion from my mind, to stop thinking about how grossed out I'd been when I'd seen his scar. There was no doubt about it—mine made his look like a scratch. I became even more self-conscious about other people seeing it.

During the competition I wore an experimental casting material produced by 3M. Created from a new combination of resins, it was easy to apply: Zack simply put a casting sock over my leg, wrapped the material around it, then added water. To take it off, he just cut it with regular scissors. It provided the stabilizing effect I needed without the cumbersome bulk—science is amazing!

With the "cast" in place, I was able to do my pommel horse routine, and did it pretty well. My strength was back; my resolve had returned, and after I was finished, I had a greater sense of accomplishment than ever before.

After the meet, I returned to Los Angeles with a new spirit: hey, I can do this! The Bull was back.

Dr. Mandelbaum, however, had a different tune. "I want you to take it easy, Tim. I don't want you pushing."

"Why?" I laughed. "It's your fault, anyway! You're the one who put the idea in my head while I was still in the hospital! You're not going to back out on me now, are you?"

He groaned. "What have I done?" He laughed.

But the worst thing was, Dr. Mandelbaum had no concrete answers for me. I kept bugging him to tell me when I'd be able to land without using the pit, whether or not my leg would be healed for the trials. Each time he X-rayed my leg he had the same comment.

"It looks good, Tim. It's coming along nicely."

That stank. I wanted specifics. I was not ready to accept the fact that medicine is such an unsure thing, that doctors don't come out of medical school with a foolproof checklist of exactly how long it will take the body to heal. What I lacked, clearly, was patience.

One day I arrived at therapy totally exhausted. Zack noticed it right away, and told me we weren't going to do our regular session.

"I can do it!' I protested. "I can't afford to stop now!" Time was marching on.

"No," he refused. "I want you to go into the therapy pool instead. You've got to take a break."

I was angry. Why were they trying to slow me down? It was almost May. We had already petitioned the USGF to have me exempt from the first trials, the USA Championships, in June, but August was not that far away. I didn't like having the reins pulled in on me.

"That pool is for old people!" I shouted at him.

"Just go, Tim. Please."

Annoyed and frustrated, I limped into the therapy pool at the UCLA Medical Center, slamming the door behind me. I'd never been in there before, and I was surprised at what I saw. The enormous pool is designed only for physical therapy use. On one side there's a ramp for wheelchairs going in and out of the water; along the width of the pool is a walkway with a railing for stabilization; there are handle grips all around the perimeter; the depth in every area is limited to a safe five feet.

The lighting was soothing, the water temperature warm. I was alone in the huge room. I took off my brace and slid into the pool. God, it felt good. I stayed there for over an hour, swimming a little, mostly lying still. My anger dissolved, and I was at peace. Zack was on my side, I knew that. So was Dr. Mandelbaum. It was time to stop taking out my frustrations on them. I'd been acting like a brat.

Throughout the past several months, Peter had come up to L.A. a few times to check on my progress. We talked frequently on the phone, and he was a great sounding board. I looked forward to seeing him at the USA Championships in Houston.

Although we had petitioned to have me exempt from the Championships, I still wanted to go through the motions of the competition. It was, after all, crunch time. I did surprisingly well, and was even able to complete both the compulsories and the optionals on the pommel horse and parallel bars.

The night after the optionals, Yefim, Peter and I went to a steak house for dinner.

Peter had some powerful words for me.

"Tim, the two events your leg didn't affect you're actually winning. Doesn't that tell you something? Your strength is back. You looked better out there than you've ever looked. You're the best you've ever been." A lot of reporters said the same thing, but, coming from Peter, I believed it.

"Now if my leg would just catch up to the rest of me . . ." I said.

"Give it time, Timmy, give it time," Yefim added.

But time was something there wasn't much of.

20

There was one month left. We stopped allowing the media into the gym; I focused on training as though it was the most important thing in the world. To me, it was.

The most difficult part was that I never knew what to expect from my leg day to day. Some days it seemed good; some days it was terribly painful. I did the best I could, though there were many skills I would have to perform at the trials that I simply didn't dare practice. When the chips were down, I knew I could do them. I knew those years of training would come back to me.

Night after night, after the others had left, Yefim and I stayed in the gym. He stretched out my leg and massaged the aching, damaged muscle. After a few minutes, he stopped.

"Okay, Yefim," I said. "I'll see you tomorrow." It had become our ritual. Yefim quietly left the gym, knowing this was my time. My time to be alone with my thoughts, in the one place I most loved to be.

I sat on the floor, continuing to stretch and massage my leg, thinking, thinking. Gymnastics was so hard for me now, and it was so painful. But in the deserted gym, where there were no distractions, I came to the realization that pain has no memory, but the experience of it can provide enough strength to last a lifetime. For me, flying through the air is the one thing I loved more than anything in the world, and it was the pleasure of it that I thought of in my solitude.

The night before we left for Salt Lake City I sat there, content with the peace. The sun was setting, its last rays spilling into the windows, catching the particles of chalk dust in the air, suspending them in a gentle, comforting way.

I feel good about what I'm doing, I thought. *No matter what happens, I have done the right thing.*

We landed in Salt Lake and I stepped off the plane. "Okay," I said to myself, "you made it. There's no turning back now."

After we checked into the hotel I went immediately to the arena. I walked over to the competition area, and, as usual, I tested the floor. Never would it have been more important for the floor to feel cushioned. It was hard as a rock. Although, with the condition of my leg, a trampoline would have felt hard as a rock. Instantly, I was discouraged, then snapped my mind back and told myself, "It'll be fine." Some habits die hard.

I roomed with Curtis—I had been right in my assumption that having to perform right after I broke my leg had been difficult for him. The day of the compulsories my brother Michael arrived. Curtis, Michael and I had lunch together, but I wasn't too talkative. I was anxious for the evening to get there; talking about it was not making it easier. I did not need to think of myself as "injured"—I needed to perceive myself as no different from the other guys: strong, healthy and competent to win.

I went back to the room and took a nap, waking up in time for the 5:00 P.M. warm-ups.

There were so many things I still hadn't done since my injury: I hadn't yet done a dismount off the high bar without the added help of an eight-inch foam mat on the floor; I had only practiced the dismount from the rings once or twice; and, most frightening of all for me, I still hadn't done the vault the way I would need to tonight.

I arrived at the arena and was glad to see my "gang": Dr. Mandelbaum was there, as was Zack. They'd become such an important part of my "support system" over these last many months.

After warm-ups my leg felt surprisingly good. This might just work, after all.

The first event in the compulsories was the rings. My arms cooperated, my neck cooperated and I had a really good routine. As I landed my dismount, my left leg buckled just a bit. Damn! I thought, though I knew my overall routine would rate a fairly high score.

Next came the floor exercise: I was really nervous about this, but I told myself I had made it through rings—now I could make it through anything. I did well here, too, though I couldn't push too hard on some skills; I just had to get through them. I got a 9.35. But it was still enough; I was getting psyched now. It was really happening. I tried not to think about the increasing soreness in my leg.

The pommel horse was next. That I knew I could do. It was the only event that hadn't been affected by my leg.

"I'm going to get a 10," I told myself.

I relaxed, confident I would do a great routine. I mounted the horse, attacked it like the old days—I was hot, and I was great. Then, when I went into my dismount, my hand slipped off the horse: an automatic fourth-tenths of a point deduction. In my entire career I had never done this. Why it happened I'll never know. I guess I was so worried about other things, about other parts of my body not performing or falling apart, I got a little careless. I still ended up with the highest score on the horse, but I was quickly discouraged. If I made a mistake on my easiest event, what would happen next?

Then came the scary one: the high bar. I gave it my all and did great—but, on the dismount, I did the compulsory back flip with a full twist and, once again, just when I thought I was going to stick it cold, my leg gave way—worse than it had on rings. The pain increased. And then, God, it was time for the vault.

"Okay, Tim," I said, "this is your moment of truth. The last time you performed this in front of an audience they carted you off on a stretcher. The only way to put it behind you is to do a good job now." This, however, was going to be a little difficult: for the first time since Rotterdam I would be doing it without a spotter and without the cushion of a softer mat. And now, after seventeen years of hurdling off my left leg to hit the springboard, I had to jump off my right. It may not seem like a big deal, but it was like all of a sudden being told you've got to write with your left hand when you're right-handed. It felt foreign; it felt awkward. And I was terrified I would screw it up.

I ran down the runway and—*pow!*—I hurdled off with my right leg. So far so good. I hit the board and flew into the air, and then I came down . . . and incredibly . . . I landed on my feet, and stuck my landing cold. I think I went into shock.

My vault, though I made it through, which for me was the most important thing, was not, however, really powerful. I knew it, and the judges knew it, too. They gave me a 9.35, which seemed low after all I'd accomplished. If they'd considered where I'd come from, I'm sure I would have scored an 11. Later, when I was talking to Bart Conner, he mentioned that the score was too low, and it confirmed my thoughts. Now at least it wasn't just me feeling sorry for myself.

Last came the parallel bars. I did great, and ended up with a 9.9. But the pain in my leg was unbearable now. I was glad the night was finished. Now I really needed the day off between the competitions.

Unfortunately, because of that stupid mistake I made on the horse, I ended up eighth—two places short of making the 1988 Olympic team. The irony didn't escape me: the pommel horse, my greatest love and the one event that hadn't been affected by my leg—making a mistake I simply never had done before, ever. Things were not going as well as I'd hoped; I would have to do better in the optionals. But even at that, I wasn't discouraged: I had come a lot farther than everyone had predicted, and I knew I was always stronger in the optionals than in the compulsories. And I would be again—if my leg held up. *If.* The big *if.*

The next morning my leg was worse. I couldn't believe it. I went to the gym only once; then it was back to bed. I needed all the rest I could get.

That night the Women's compulsories were held. I went to the arena to watch, and was struck by one grim thought: there was going to be a lot of heartache at these trials. Besides me, Dan Hayden had a difficult time at the compulsories; now our top woman gymnast only a few years ago, Sabrina Mar, was having back problems. Kristie Phillips and Doe Yamashiro were not doing well, either—it seemed as though the bodies of all the top U.S. gymnasts were betraying them.

I went to bed that night, trying not to think about the next day. In the morning, I opened my eyes, conscious of only one thing: I was in tremendous pain.

I spent the day in and out of the Jacuzzi, constantly rubbing my leg, trying, trying so hard to loosen it up. I went to Yefim's room: he massaged it, stretched it. We hardly talked—there was nothing to say.

I got to the arena early for 5:00 P.M. warm-ups. My leg was no better. We did some ice massage and applied an electric stimulator. That helped a little, very little.

We were going to start on floor exercise, and I still didn't know what routine I was going to do. Obstinate as I had always been to stick to my prepared routine, there was no way. I had planned to do a pass that included a front handspring to a one-and-three-quarters front flip rolling out, similar to the way a diver slices into the water, but which would have to end up with me standing on my feet. *Both* feet. I was afraid if I didn't hit the floor hard enough after the handspring I wouldn't rotate enough for the flip. If that happened, I could very easily land on my head and kill myself. During warm-ups I kept trying to do an alternative, lesser skill, but it wasn't working. I just didn't have enough time.

I went through warm-ups on all the other apparatus, then went back to the floor. The alternative skill still wasn't working.

"Well, Tim, you're probably going to die," I told myself, convinced I was going to have to give my original plan a shot. I practiced the handspring over and over, inflicting more and more abuse on my aching leg, as I pounded it into the mat.

It happened suddenly—I decided this was not worth dying for. I tried the alternative skill again. It was so-so. I knew I might not make it, but at least I wouldn't get killed.

By now, I could hardly walk. The competition began.

My name was called, and I saluted the judge. I don't think I've ever been more scared in my life: not in Rotterdam, not even with Annie, the ax-lady. On my first pass I went into a flip and punched it. It was then that I felt a very strange sensation in my leg, not so much of pain but of an instability. I stood up and put pressure on my leg. I thought I had broken it again. I ended up with a 9.0 for the routine; I needed a 9.2

I limped off the floor and went to Yefim.

"It was the best I could do," I said.

He patted my shoulder. "That's fine, Timmy. Get ready for pommel horse."

The pommel horse. My greatest love. Suddenly the competition faded away, and what I was about to do next became important only to me. This routine now represented more than another gymnastics event—I wanted it to be the thing I'll remember when I'm ninety-five.

I put my all into it, and when I landed, I almost said, "Okay. You did it. You did the thing you love more than anything in the world. And you did it good. And it's okay. Everything's going to be okay." I scored a 9.9.

The crowd was incredible. I can never remember receiving such an ovation—not at the Olympics, not anywhere—that had such a depth of feeling behind it. That made me go on, and helped me get through the next event, the rings.

But the rings were to be my last event: I landed poorly. A bolt of pain shot through my leg, then exploded through my entire body. It was now more than obvious that my body was just not going to hold together.

I sat on the sidelines with Yefim and Dr. Mandelbaum. Then I said the most difficult words of my life.

"I don't think I should go on, Yefim. What do you think?"

"I don't know, Timmy, how do you feel?"

Right up until the end, he knew it had to be my decision. He knew this was the moment I would live with for the rest of my life.

"I feel it's over," I said quietly.

Dr. Mandelbaum put his hand on my arm.

"You've done what you set out to do, Tim. You've already won. You're here. And you did great," he said, then added, "You can go home now."

Slowly, I began to unwind my tired-out wrist wraps. The edges were frayed, traces of adhesive puckered the end. I thought about how far these pieces of cotton had brought me, about the memories they would hold forever in their fibers. I was so grateful that Yefim had not let them be cut off in Rotterdam.

I put on my warm-up jacket. I wanted to leave the arena, but I didn't want the people to think I was bitter. I leaned on Yefim for support. Suddenly, with the competition still going on, there was an uncomfortable silence in the arena. Then the crowd stood and applauded me. Somehow, they knew. I wanted to hide my head, but I had to look up at them—they were so kind, they seemed to really feel my sadness. I could not stop my tears, as I looked at their knowing faces, and I said, simply, "Thank you."

Afterward, ABC's Frank Gifford summed up the emotion when he said:

"It is not often that the end of a career is so obvious, and so sudden. Usually it's something private. A decision reached through reflection and sometimes pain. But during the Olympic Trials, in full view of the public, Tim Daggett's career ended. The final act was swift, raw and honest. But Tim Daggett went out the way he wanted, doing what he loved most, the way he most loved to do it."

At the end of the competition it is traditional for all the athletes to go out onto the floor and line up. Then the new Olympic team, standing across from those who didn't make it, is introduced. As badly as I was feeling, emotionally and physically, I wanted to be there. Seventeen years of my life were going to be concluded the right way.

They introduced each member: first place, second, third, fourth, fifth. When they got to the sixth place member—the last qualifying place to make the competing team—they introduced Dominic Minagucci, a kid who never thought he'd make it. As they said his name he burst into tears.

I watched him, filled with the knowing that if I had made the team, he wouldn't have. I saw the joy in his tear-filled eyes, and felt every quiver of his trembling body.

"That was me in 1984," I said to myself. And I knew everything really would be okay. I cried, too, not for myself this time, but for Dominic. I was so happy for him. It was time for his dream to come true—it was his time now, mine had passed.

When the ceremonies were closing, Peter appeared at the microphone. I knew he had been in the audience, but was surprised to see him standing there.

"They've asked me to say a few words about someone very special here tonight," he began.

Oh, no, I suddenly thought. I sensed what was coming. My gut tightened. I couldn't go through this.

"Together, Tim Daggett and I shared a dream. Together, we saw that dream come true. As we recognize the new team members tonight, we feel it's also important to recognize another element of greatness—Tim's. He has showed us true courage, true spirit and true guts. He is a credit to our sport, to the highest degree." Peter's voice cracked a little as he said his closing words. "And I, for one, am proud to call him my friend."

The crowd cheered, the ceremonies ended. I walked over to Peter, my eyes filled with tears.

"You know, I really love you, man," I said.

He reached over and gave me a hug.

It was over.

EPILOGUE
To Dream Again

It was time to go home: home to West Springfield. I was leaving behind many friends, many memories, but home was where I belonged. So much had happened since I'd left over eight years before. I had traveled the world, received recognition beyond belief and made lifelong bonds with people from all over the globe. And more than that, I had seen all my dreams come true. I had not given up the struggle; and because of that, I felt I was a winner.

But I wanted to go back to my roots. I had spent so much time away from my family—now I wanted to be with them, to try to make up for the lost time, and for the sacrifices they had all made for me.

I also knew now that I would never—could never—be far from a gym, and that I wanted to help kids, kids who were just like I'd been, kids from small-town America. Coach Jones had recently retired from the high school and, along with former Springfield College gymnast Joe Saimeri, had opened a private gym. I wanted to work with Coach again, this time being the one hopefully to train and inspire kids the way he had trained and inspired me. I feel a great need to take one kid all the way—to show him how he, too, can hear that Olympic theme song play in his head and, one day, have his dream come true.

I cleaned out my apartment in L.A. and went for one last walk around the campus. I went into the old gym where we had practiced during my first year here . . . there was still a hole in the wall where I'd made the plaster come tumbling down; I walked the stairs I had run up and down countless times while training; I walked past the dorms, up Bruin Walk where I had first realized I "could make it, too"; I went to Pauley Pavilion and relived the images of that golden night.

I had one more stop before leaving: I went to the John Wooden Center, where we had trained for the Olympics. I stood in the emptiness, seeing the apparatus in my mind, feeling once again the grueling days of workouts, the exhausting, exhilarating practice, day after day, night after night. And then, in my mind, I heard Peter's voice echo throughout the hollow gym.

"Next up for the USA, Tim Daggett on high bar. He needs a perfect 10 for the team to beat the Chinese . . ."

I smiled at the memories, so real, so full. I turned and limped quietly off the floor: I was done. The threads of my life would always be here, but it was time for life to go on.

This time I did not fly home amid the flurry in airports and crowds of well-wishers. I calmly got into my car, put on my seat belt, got on the Santa Monica Freeway, and headed east.

Soon after the trials I had the opportunity to go on a "Celebrity Cruise" as a guest of Norwegian Lines. The cruises are wonderful: you spend a week mingling with the guests and having a great time. They gave me two tickets.

Because my family has always been foremost in my life, I wanted to take one of my brothers or sisters, but there were six of them . . . and only one extra ticket! As most large families know, there's only one fair way to do things . . . so . . . we held a lottery!

We put the six names into a hat: Michael. Susan. Sharon. Daniel. David. Sheila. We were crammed into the kitchen, with my mother watching over us in case a referee was needed. I picked the winning name: it was Sharon.

"I demand a recount!" David yelled.

"You can't have a recount in a lottery!" Daniel said.

To this day, because she wasn't there when we did it, my sister Susan is convinced we never put in her name! Not true! Sharon and I were off to the Caribbean, and we had a fabulous time. It was a vacation which, for me, was long overdue.

With gymnastics competition behind me, I now had to seriously start thinking about what I was going to do. I made some appearances—including "The Oprah Winfrey Show"—and I received the high honor of being named "Athlete of the Year" by the New York Athletic Club, where I was introduced by Donald Trump. I began traveling the country (more planes!) again, this time giving my motivational talk not to the press, but to countless businesses and organizations. Among these talks was one I gave to a banquet sponsored by IBM, called "Salute to Youth," for a group of about 250 high school seniors and their parents in upstate New York.

After my speech I was signing autographs, when one girl came up to me. "I've been going through some tough times myself," she said. "Not with gymnastics—I'm not much of an athlete—but with my life. I just wanted to thank you for all you said tonight. You really helped me get my head together."

I signed the back of her program and she left. But with her words she had shown me my own direction: it was then that I discovered I could help others deal with their problems through sharing the ones I had gone through. I loved speaking to audiences; it was not unlike performing once again. And if, on top of that, I could actually *help* people, help motivate them to realize *their* dreams, well, suddenly I knew what my new career was meant to be.

My dream had changed and had now become two: to coach kids in gymnastics, and to try to motivate people from all walks of life. Finding that direction for me didn't really take a lot of thought: I guess it was there all along. The new dreams will never be the same as making it to the 1984 Olympics, but the challenges will still be there—new, exciting challenges.

In December I had been asked to do some publicity and a pommel horse exhibition at the U.S./USSR meet in nearby Worcester, Massachusetts. I wanted to be a small part of the performance, and also, I wanted to see Dmitri.

I was inside the hotel, walking through the lobby, when my head turned, as if by a magnet, to the front door. There he was. Our eyes met. I smiled. He raised his hands for victory. I raised mine for friendship. He shrugged with sympathy. I nodded. Across the bustling lobby, we quietly conversed with our hands and with our eyes. It was our common language, and we understood each other perfectly. The "knowing" between us ran deep.

Soon after that, I received another prestigious honor: I was asked to become an athlete representative to the board of directors for the U.S. Gymnastics Federation. This meant I would still be close to the sport I had dedicated seventeen years of my life to, and perhaps now I could play a meaningful role in shaping the future of our nation's gymnasts. It also meant I would need to be present at all major meets.

The first competition I went to after the trials was the NCAA Championships in April 1989. For the first time, I was in the stands. It was with a feeling of sadness that I watched the guys from UCLA compete without me.

Jim Mikus was there, and I was glad to see my long-ago friend. He sat in the stands beside me and, of course, we talked about my leg. Then he said something that was, at first, very unsettling.

"I'm glad you didn't make it to Seoul, Tim," he said.

I couldn't believe this was my friend talking. But as he continued, I knew what he meant.

"You've got the rest of your life ahead of you now. If you'd gone to Seoul, the focus would have shifted totally onto your triumph there.

And what was really important to you—the struggle—would have been lost along the way."

And then it all began to make sense. I thought about the changes I had had to make in my life, and about where I was now. With Jim's words, I came to terms with the fact that dreams don't always come true with a fanfare of flowers and a gold medal wrapped around your neck. Sometimes dreams come true on the inside. And that's when they become even more special. I would never forget winning the gold; but more than that, I would never forget my *goals*. And I would always know I had been true to myself.

Shortly after the meet, these thoughts were reconfirmed by a letter that appeared in *USA Gymnastics* magazine. It was written by one of the kids I am now coaching, Ali Eslami. At nine-years-old, Ali had this, in part, to say:

"My favorite gymnast is Tim Daggett. I love to think about Tim's motivational speech that I heard one night. I will never forget his speech for the rest of my life. Whenever I think about the words he spoke, it makes me work harder to reach my goals."

Man, this is what life's all about.

In between speaking engagements and coaching "my kids," I also spent much of the summer of 1989 visiting various gymnastics camps, and performing in exhibitions. At one camp, a little girl came up to me and asked for my autograph. Obviously too young to remember the excitement of 1984, she had been told that I had received a gold medal.

She looked up at me with huge blue eyes and asked innocently, "But did you ever get any big trophies?" As much as my daily workouts kept my dream in focus, this kind of encounter today helps me keep things in perspective.

I speak to Peter often, and I stay in touch with the other guys from time to time. I think we probably always will. The kind of bond that we shared together simply doesn't go away overnight.

On July 31, 1989, I was on a boat with some friends, waterskiing and having some fun—things I'd not had enough of for so many years. Suddenly I looked at my watch and noticed the date. Wow. Tonight was the fifth anniversary of winning the gold. I mentioned it to them, and we talked about it a while. Then, as the sunset forced us off the river, our conversation drifted to other things.

It never occurred to me that anyone else but my family and closest friends would be aware of what the date meant to me, but later that night I heard that the local television station had done a piece on the anniversary. The sports commentator said: "We don't know where Tim Daggett is right now, or what he's doing, but we can be sure that today—at least once—he's remembered what the date is. Happy Anniversary, Tim, wherever you are."

My hometown had not forgotten.

It was a little hard to believe when that five-year milestone passed; soon it was six years, then seven. During this time I've had many more wonderful experiences: my motivational speaking has enabled me to meet and share my thoughts about "overcoming obstacles" with business and salespeople from corporations and associations throughout the country; my television gymnastics commentary has afforded me the opportunity to keep on top of the sport I love so much; and coaching "my kids" has given me the chance to spend time in the one place that I will always call home—a gym.

In January of 1990 Coach Jones, Joe Saimeri, and I renamed our gym *Tim Daggett Gold Medal Gymnastics*, and in the fall of 1991 we built a new world-class training facility in Agawam, Massachusetts. It is here that I hope to help the goals of young gymnasts grow into reality, and to show them that nothing in life is impossible, as long as they dare to dream. I have seen it work for myself; I have seen it work for others, young and old alike.

I still work out regularly, not just to keep in shape for my exhibitions, but also because I want to stay as healthy as possible. In fact, I even still run—not that one mile every day—but I run as often as I can, usually with some of my brothers and sisters and Susan's husband, Scott. The other day we decided to run at the high school, where there are great hills that really make you work at it. We ran down one hill, then up another, then down the one that runs alongside the "Tim Daggett Gymnasium."

"How dare you guys run by this without saluting?" I laughingly criticized.

"Are you kidding?" asked my sister Sharon.

"Give us a break," Scott said.

"Get real," Sheila added.

Well, I guess the glory days are behind me now. But beneath it all, I know I have what's really important: the love of my family, the knowledge that I have succeeded, and the experience to know that if I give it everything I've got, I can make the dreams for the rest of my life come true.

We circled around the gym and headed back up the hill. In my heart, I saluted.

My Brothers and Sisters—What Became of Them?

Michael—Graduated with a Psychology degree from American International College, Springfield, Massachusetts; he currently sells commercial insurance.

Susan—After high school, she went to work in the family business ("She had to help support us little kids!" David says—and the others agree); now she works for a dentist, and is the mother of a son, Ryan Scott Parent, born July 11, 1990.

Scott Parent (Susan's husband)—Graduated from Holyoke Community College, Holyoke, Massachusetts; he currently works in paper sales.

Sharon—Received an Education degree from the University of Massachusetts, Amherst, and a Masters degree in Education from American International College; she currently teaches third grade in the Springfield Public Schools.

David—Received a Psychology degree from the University of Massachusetts, Amherst; he now works in sales for an electronics firm.

Daniel—Received an Economics degree from the University of Massachusetts, Amherst; he currently is doing graduate work in Marketing, and is employed in the pension department of an insurance company.

Sheila—Graduated from the University of Massachusetts, Amherst, School of Nursing; she works now as a Registered Nurse.